PRAISE
Is What I Do!
NO OTHER OPTION

O'Neal Porter

PRAISE IS WHAT I DO
NO OTHER OPTION

O'Neal Porter

Oh Kneel Publishing

Unless otherwise indicated all Scripture quotations are taken from the King James Version of the Holy Bible. Please note that **Oh Kneel Publishing Company's** publishing style capitalizes pronouns in Scripture that refer to the Father, Son, and Holy Spirit, and may differ from some Bible publishers' styles.

Praise Is What I Do – No Other Option
Copyright 2006 by Oh Kneel Publishing
P.O. Box 13125
Eight Mile, Alabama 36633
(251) 219-4327
ohkneelpublishing@yahoo.com

Printed in the United States of America. All rights reserved under International Copyright Law. Contents and/or cover may not be reproduced in whole or part in any form without the expressed written consent of the Publisher.

CONTENTS

	PAGE
DEDICATION	7
INTRODUCTION	9
NO OTHER OPTION	17
A YET PRAISE	23
ADVERSITY - A CALLING CARD	31
AN ATTITUDE ADJUSTMENT	39
IS THERE A RIGHT PLACE?	47
WHEN IS THE RIGHT TIME?	55
WORD-BASED PRAISE	65
WHEN I ROSE THIS MORNING	77
A REAL PRAISE	85
WHEN I THINK OF THE GOODNESS	95
POWER IN PRAISE	101
THERE IS A PLACE	111
OUT OF YOUR COMFORT ZONE	117
PRAISE IN SPITE OF YOURSELF	125
PRAISE - THE NATURAL THING TO DO	131
HOW TO DO IT	137
PRAISE AND FAITH	142
ABOUT THE AUTHOR	148

DEDICATION

To God be the glory, for the great and marvelous things He has done! Words are insufficient to express my gratitude for God's mercy, grace, and favor that He has bestowed upon me down through the years and even now. This book is the product of many tears, much sweat, many trials, much pain and for it all, I give God the glory. This book is only the beginning of much more that I believe God has invested in me and impressed upon me to share with the Body of Christ and even to those who have not come to the knowledge of the Son of God as their Lord and Savior.

Sabrina, thank you for sharing twenty plus years of your life with me. Thank you for being a part of my dreams, my desires and especially my destiny.

To Daddy's "golden guineas": Kymberly Dawnique, Brooke O'Neal, Morgan Char'les, Charles Van James, I pray that you always know how special you are to your father and I thank you for sharing me with others that I may minister unto the masses.

I thank my parents, Rev. Charles (Joyce) Porter and Harriet Stallworth Moore for their love and unselfish support of me through the good times, bad times, happy times and sad times. I pray that you are pleased and proud.

To my extended biological family, my spiritual family (especially the saints at Fellowship Church), my pastor Dr. W.E. Jones, my mentors and my friends (I won't start calling names) thank you for loving me unconditionally and supporting me continuously.

To the readers, I pray that this is a blessing and encouragement for you!

INTRODUCTION

For years, I have taught the church that "life will be life." What exactly does that mean? It simply means that life is filled with good and bad, ups and downs, smiles and frowns, successes and failures, positives and negatives. It does not matter what your level of spirituality is, life still happens.

> When the foundation is built deep in the Word of God, then the structure can weather storms – even hurricanes!

Natural disasters. Sickness and disease. Terrorist attacks. Gang violence. Drug abuse. Divorce. Teenage pregnancy. Racial discrimination. War. Poverty.

These are not far off or far away occurrences. They are real events that we are challenged with everyday. Hurricane Katrina, September 11 (9-11), the war in Iraq, and to bring it even closer – your friend with AIDS, your cousin whose marriage failed, your aunt with cancer, your child on drugs, your employment that is uncertain, the crack addict on the corner, the little boy whose father just died, the mother struggling to raise her children as a single parent. Some of these are issues that even your own household has to deal with on a daily basis.

Some people have the notion that if they just start going to church, pay their tithes, learn and do all the spiritual rituals that everything will be alright. Well, I have a rude awakening for you. Doing those things will not make "everything alright." Usually, when a person begins to do those things sincerely from the heart, it infuriates the devil. And when he gets mad, he intensifies his job description found in **John 10:10**, *"to steal, kill and destroy."* However, as Christians we do not have to fret over the devil's actions, because Jesus promised in the same verse that He *"came to bring life and life more abundantly."*

As Christians, we must be prepared to handle the challenges of life and not allow life to overwhelm us. It does not matter how spiritually deep you are or how heavenly high you may be, you must still understand the facts of this life. Good things happen to bad people. And, bad things happen to good people. In **Matthew 5:45** the Scriptures declare: *"...for He maketh His sun to rise on the evil and on the good, and sendeth rain on the just and* *the unjust."* So, there is nothing that you or I can do to prevent some things in life from occurring. Life will still present challenges on a daily basis, including: divorce, loss of job, drug addiction, abuse, infirmities, family problems, discrimination, death, fears, and the list is endless. The presence of these issues does not denote what type person you are. However, the key for Christians is how you allow these "life issues" to affect you.

There is a wonderful parable in the Word of God found in **Matthew 7:24-27**.

"Therefore whosoever heareth these sayings of mine, and doeth them, I will liken him unto a wise man, which built his house upon a rock: And the rain descended, and the floods came, and the winds blew, and beat upon that house; and it fell not; for it was founded upon a rock. And everyone that heareth these sayings of Mine, and doeth them not, shall be likened unto a foolish man, which built his house upon the sand: And the rain descended, and the floods came, and the winds blew, and beat upon that house; and it fell: and great was the fall of it."

People are just like those two houses. Some are built on spiritual and emotional beachfront property. They look good. They sound good. They have the outward appearance of being all they need to be. They have learned how to *"do their dance"*. And their *"tongue language"* is heavenly sounding. But, when all hell breaks loose, they fall apart? Why? The reason is the foundation. If you have not allowed your spirit and soul to be built and strengthened by the truth of God's Word, you will not stand in the time of storm.

There are so many church people who have fallen away because of a poor and unstable foundation. The storms of life (death, illness, divorce, unemployment, drug abuse, fear, etc.) have come and swept them away. God created us to withstand storms. He created us with purpose and destiny within us to stand firm. He invested His Word as our foundation and strength. But, some people have not allowed the Word to fall on good ground in their life so they may experience and see the benefits of the manifested Word of God. So, what looked good for a season could not stand the scrutiny of the storm. However, when the foundation is built deep in the Word of God, the structure can weather storms – even hurricanes! There are many Christians who have battled the spirit of poverty and are yet standing. There are praying saints who have lost loved ones to infirmity and disease, but their faith has remained intact. There are Christians who have battled addictions and abuse, but they have come out victorious. The real effect that God wants storms to have on our lives is to strengthen our faith, and not weaken our walk.

God has purposed that there is a remnant. Yes, there are those who have determined to hold fast to their faith and stand on the Word of God. No matter which way the wind blows, there are those who have learned to withstand the elements. In **Romans 8:35-39**, Paul describes such a people.

"Who shall separate us from the love of Christ? Shall tribulation, or distress, or persecution, or famine, or nakedness, or peril, or sword? As it is written, For Thy sake we are killed all the day long; we are accounted as sheep for the slaughter. Nay, in all these things we are more than conquerors through Him that loved us. For I am persuaded, that neither death, nor life, nor angels, nor principalities, nor powers, nor things present, nor things to come, nor height, nor

depth, nor any other creature, shall be able to separate us from the love of God, which is in Christ Jesus our Lord."

Life offers so many challenges, obstacles, adversities, and the list goes on and on. This reminds me of the scripture verses: *"Man that is born of a woman is of a few days, and those are full of trouble,"* **(Job 14:1)** and *"Many are the afflictions of the righteous, but the Lord delivereth us out of them all.* **(Psalm 34:19)"** The Scriptures have prepared us to realize that everyday will not be sunny. We will have some storm clouds and raindrops sometimes. But, our attitude must be – it takes rain in order to grow. When life gives you lemons, rejoice and make delicious lemon-aid. There is nothing that life can offer, that the power of God is not able to bring victory.

It is easy to smile when the sun is shining. When the bills are paid and there is still money left over, it is not difficult to be elated. When the doctor's report is a clean bill of health, it is not a hard thing to be worry-free. When the spouse is loving and caring and the children are obedient and respectful, it is no problem to be happy. But, what do you do when life offers a different picture? How do you respond when all hell is breaking loose in your life? What do you do when you experience what Paul writes about in Corinthians "We are troubled on every side" – but you (in contrast to the Scripture) are stressed out? "Confused" and you are in despair?

There is a key to surviving life! It is a spiritual key. You must cause your spirit man to be in charge of your soulish man and flesh. You cannot just let your emotions get the best of you. You must even dismiss your "five senses" and allow faith to kick in and begin to operate. You must allow the wisdom and revelation that God deposits in your heart to control the actions of your mind and body.

God has provided a way to bring His glory into what seems like a "hell-filled" life. Remember, the old hymn "Blessed assurance, Jesus is mine, Oh what a foretaste of glory divine…" When the Spirit of Christ takes His rightful place in your life things will change. When the knowledge of the Word of God takes preeminence in your life, things will change. I know that many Christians struggle everyday. Sometimes, you may feel like giving up. Sometimes it seems as though you have already lost the battle. Sometimes the devil is talking so loud, you can't hear anything else. When nothing works! When everything goes wrong! What do you do? **Praise is what I do! No Other Option.**

NO OTHER OPTION

The sub-caption in the title of this book may stir a bit of controversy. Some may feel that there are other options. I beg to differ. If we keep in context the subjects of the title, there is no other option for Christians. First of all, Christians have been bought with a price and are not their own. Secondly, Christians are being conformed into the image of the Son daily. Thirdly, Christians' purpose for living is to glorify and please God.

> Praise dictates the posture of our body and our soul. We stand when others fall. We bounce back when others never recover. We smile when others frown. We think ourselves happy, when others resolve to be sad.

With these thoughts in mind, Christians have no other option but to "praise" God.

If I was referring only to those who are simply religious, then there might be other options. If I was discussing hypocrites or sinners, then there would be other options. If I was talking about backsliders or carnal individuals, then other options would be a choice. However, I am not talking about any of those persons.

Romans 14:23 says "...*Whatsoever is not of faith is sin.*" The context of this particular verse of scripture deals specifically with the liberty of Christians in regards to how they live before unbelievers. Every action that we take must be done to God's glory. And, we must learn to respect others' individualism. God is such a personal God that he can appreciate the praise of one swinging from a chandelier just as much as He can from one seated and gently waving their hand in the air. The bottom line is that what we have with God must be true to our heart. We must have a relationship with others that clearly demonstrates our unwavering faith in God and relentless praise and worship of our God.

I recall the funeral services for the late Coretta Scott King. Her daughter, Elder Bernice King, made a statement that demonstrated the strength, courage, faith, and posture that true believers must exhibit even in times of sorrow. She referred to the 150th Psalm and encouraged everyone present at that homegoing celebration to praise God. "Everything that hath breath, Praise ye the Lord." That is the only option we have in times of grief, sorrow, discouragement, challenge, dismay, or whatever may betide.

Since we (as Christians) have been bought with a price we do not belong to ourselves [or the devil] at all. As obedient Christians we surrender our will to God's will. We sacrifice our fleshly desires to obey His spiritual will. **I Corinthians 6:20** reminds us: *"For ye are bought with a price: therefore glorify God in your body, and in your spirit, which are God's."* So, we have no other option but to praise God in our body. For we understand, that our body does not even belong to us. Our hands, our lips, our feet, our every thing belongs to God. We must make every effort to praise God with our complete body, soul and spirit.

Secondly, if we are being conformed daily into the image of the Son, we must line up with who the Son is and what the Son does. The "WWJD" fad that was so popular a few years ago, served as an excellent reminder to help us conform into the image of the Son. Just think about it, each time you are faced with a challenge, you ask yourself, "What Would Jesus Do?" **Romans 8:29** addresses our destiny, *"For whom He did foreknow, He also did predestinate to be conformed to the image of His Son, that He might be the firstborn among many brethren."* God wants us to study His Word and change ourselves daily into the image of our elder brother, Jesus Christ. Our walk must change. Our talk must change. Our relationships must change. Our decisions and actions must change.

We cannot *"Be Like Mike"*. But, we must strive to be like Jesus. Society has built up so many images that we struggle to assimilate to, but these are not the images that God desires. We must remind ourselves that our response of praise dictates the posture of our body and our soul. We stand when others fall. We bounce back when others never recover. We smile when others frown. We think ourselves happy, when others resolve to be sad.

And finally, we must realize that our purpose for existing is simply to glorify God. **Psalm 102:18** declares, **"This shall be written for the generation to come: and the people which shall be created shall praise the LORD."** Our total existence should be to bring glory to the Father. Every waking moment we should see ourselves as ambassadors (representatives) of the kingdom of heaven. The Bible even says that we are aliens here. We should not be so comfortable with the ways of this world that we begin to pattern ourselves after it. But, we must realize that we have been sent here by God. And while on assignment here on earth, we must represent the one who sent us well. So, in everything we do and say, God should be glorified. We thank Him in good times and in bad times. We praise Him in happy times and sad times. We honor Him in sickness and in health. At all times, for all things, and in everything, we must give praise, honor and glory to the Father. There is no other option.

When we allow other options to become part of the puzzle, we step out of the will of God. When there are other options, what we are saying is that we don't trust that our God is able. When there are other options, we are expressing a lack of gratitude for what He has done and a lack of confidence in what He can do. When there are other options, we have abandoned our faith and we have virtually become our own gods.

A YET PRAISE

A very dear friend of mine lay in a hospital bed in the final stages of cancer. Her body was worn and fragile from the awesome fight. Yet, her spirit and soul were strong as ever. She refused to give up. She would not let go her faith. And that is what manifested in her final actions. The marvelous thing that I will never forget is how even when she lost her ability to speak effectively, she would gurgle out the word, "Hallelujah". She could have just cried or lay there, but she was a prayer warrior and a praiser. Instead of fretting or complaining, she maintained her faith in God. She set the perfect example of how to endure a physical challenge and yet keep your spirit and soul intact.

> When difficult times come, I want to get close to the One and only One who can bring the true deliverance I really need.

I have seen so many people who have had to face challenges in their body, and they were bitter. They were angry. They were angry with God and anyone who would come in their presence. Their anger manifested against their caregivers, family, and anyone who would cross their path. I have never understood why some people do not consider their blessings in spite of their challenges. It is not like we have earned an exemption for trouble. **Job 14:1** states, *"Man that is born of a woman is of a few days, and full of trouble."* So, it seems that since we understand that trouble is going to come regardless, we should simply prepare ourselves for it and continue to walk in victory. **Psalm 34:19** even declares that *"Many are the afflictions of the righteous."* So, it does not bother me to know that afflictions, trials, peril, storm, all shall come. For I have learned to rest on the knowledge that *"God is delivering us out of them all."* Hallelujah! Thank you Jesus! So, I yet praise Him. In spite of how it looks, how it seems or how it feels.

    That is what a yet praise is. It is a consistent, deliberate, intentional, unwavering, determined acknowledgement of and excitement about God regardless of what is going on. Storms of life may come, but I will yet praise Him. Trouble and trials may show up, but I will yet praise Him. Money may get funny, but I will yet praise Him. Family and friends may forsake me, but I will yet praise Him.

My praise is not based upon my blessings. I always tell people that if God did nothing for you at all, He is worthy to be praised just because He is God! We are appreciative that God is a healer, a deliverer, a comforter, a way maker, and the list goes on. Yet, my praise is based upon the fact that God is God. God is God all by Himself. There is none like unto Him. He is good and righteous. So, irregardless of what I see, feel, or experience, I can yet praise Him.

In the days in which we live, many Christians are being challenged with infirmities and disease as never before. Some people have the opinion that when someone becomes sick, it is because they are out of the will of God. Or if they don't miraculously get up off their sick bed, then they have no faith. That is not true. I believe in divine healing. I believe in supernatural intervention. But, what we must keep at the forefront of our mind is that no matter what we face - God is still God. That's right! He is Jehovah Rapha, the God that healeth us.

What we must really look at is the big picture. Many times when we are faced with challenges we try and focus on ourselves. But, when we look at God's purpose and plan – much of what we go through is not even about us.

I am reminded about the man who had been lame from birth **(John 9:1-3)**. The disciples began to question Jesus and asked who sinned? And Jesus quickly responded that this was done for God's glory. Yes, many of our challenges are opportunities for God to get the glory. I believe it happens because God has faith in us. Just like He had faith in Job, I believe that God believes in us. God believes that we will "yet" praise Him.

Yes, we must learn to ignore our situations, circumstances, and conditions and began to glorify God even the more. The enemy brings distractions to our life to try and pull us away from God. But, we must learn to allow "life issues" to draw us nearer to God. That's right, when difficult times come, I want to get close to the One and only One who can bring the true deliverance I need. And, my attitude as I patiently wait on God must be the same as the Hebrew boys. I know that God will deliver me, but if He doesn't deliver me, it does not mean that He can't.

In my own life, I've faced many challenges and obstacles. As a child, I endured many things that I could have used as an excuse not to be successful. I went through sexual, physical and emotional abuse. But, instead of allowing those horrible situations to be stumbling blocks, I made them stepping stones. In the words of the songwriter,

"I've had some good days, I've had some hills to climb, I've had some weary days, and lonely nights..." But, all of that really does not matter because my heart is fixed and my mind is made up to give God the glory regardless.

That is a choice that I have made. That's right, I choose to be blessed. I choose to be happy. I choose to smile. I choose to praise God. It is a conscious decision. I do it on purpose. When my back has been against the wall, I simply have learned to stand there and begin to praise God.

One night I was restless. I tossed and I turned. I was facing a serious life issue the next day and did not know how it was going to turn out. The issue was not caused by the devil, but my own irresponsibility with my personal finances. I was about to lose a bedroom set, computer and other personal items I had in storage. Fear was gripping my mind because there were legal documents contained as well. I had almost given up hope. As I wrestled in my mind, the Spirit of God that was deep in my belly rose up through the depression, through the grief, through the hurt, through the agony, through the pain and gave me direction. I got up out of my bed and I went to the bathroom. I turned on the light and looked in the mirror. I began to talk to God. I spoke confidently because there was no other place to go and nothing else to do. I explained to God that I could not handle this and I simply gave it over to Him. Sounds easy, but it takes a lot of will power and mental strength to honestly release problems and burdens.

After standing there and releasing everything into God's hands, I began to thank and praise God in advance for the victory. I went back and laid down in the bed and told God how much I loved him and I how much I appreciated Him. Also, I told him I was going to sleep because I knew that He could handle what I could not. And, oh the rest and peace I experienced that night was unexplainable. The "peace that passeth all understanding" discussed in the Book of Philippians was actually keeping my heart and my mind.

Did the devil try and shake my faith? Of course he did. That is his job. The word of God declares in **John 10:10**, that *"the thief cometh not but for to steal, kill, and destroy."* But, my focus had already been changed. So, it did not matter to me that the devil was trying to make me doubt God. In my mind, I ran over to the Book of James, where the Bible declares *"If you resist the devil, he will flee."* That is exactly what I did. I began to ignore the thoughts, images, fears, and despair that the devil attempted to flood my mind. Instead, I flooded my mind with praise, worship, thanksgiving, faith and hope.

The next day arrived and God woke me with new mercies on my mind. Not only did I feel good, but God's favor began to make good things come my way. My entire day was blessed as God solved the problem and blessed me on top of it. I was able to recover all of my property. My legal documents were secure and in place and had not been tampered with. The people were actually even nice to me, after experiencing a very different attitude on the phone a few days earlier. Ain't God awesome?

It was my attitude that set me up to be blessed. Because I had already decided to praise God regardless, faith had to kick in and bring victory my way. A "yet" praise will bring you through everytime. When things look bad – offer a "yet" praise. When things ARE BAD, offer a "yet" praise. When your body and mind don't want to praise, sacrificially give a "yet" praise.

I am reminded of David in **Psalm 103** where he commanded his soul to bless God. He reminded his soul of all of God's benefits. He reminded himself how God was a healer, a deliverer, a way maker, a blessor. He had no choice but to bless the Lord. We must do the same. God has been better than good to each of us. So, we must ignore our feelings and our condition and "yet" praise God!

ADVERSITY: A CALLING CARD

Adversity seems to be a calling card for praise. Silent voices and stilled emotions come to life when trouble comes. It should not be so, but many people have a *"911 relationship"* with God. In times of crisis, emergency, peril, storm, or trouble people cry out to God. At these times they are crying out for help. Seeking the presence of God becomes so crucial.

> The more knowledge of the Word of God you have, the more battles you can successfully win against the enemy.

I think about people praying. Some people feel inadequate to pray, especially in public. Just ask them to pray before choir rehearsal or at the beginning of Sunday School – and you would think that you had asked them to do an impossible feat. However, isn't it strange when trouble comes, these same people know how to wail, weep, mourn, cry, and petition God!

That of course is not the will or plan of God. His ultimate desire is to have the fellowship as mentioned by the songwriter, *"And He walks with me, and He talks with me, and He tells me I am His own..."* God desires a daily, intimate fellowship with man. When we develop a continual fellowship with God: some storms are bypassed and others are endured unawares.

God's presence can cause the enemy to flee. God and His Word are the same. David wrote, **"Hide your Word in my heart, that I may not sin against Thee."** God's Word has power. When we learn God's Word and use God's Word, the devil has to flee. The enemy does not like the challenges of God's Word. The devil has no power or authority when a believer fervently and effectively mixes his or her prayer with faith by standing on the Word of God. Jesus is our primary example in demonstrating how to utilize the Word of God for our benefit.

Jesus had just returned from a 40-day fast. Of course his physical body was hungry, tired, and weak. But his spirit man was strong, vibrant, and energized. He countered the devil on every attempt by using the Word of God as a weapon. You and I must operate the same way. We can bypass many negative situations in our life by allowing the Word of God to defeat the devil. The Word has power.

When we use the Word, will the devil go away and never return? Not quite! For the Scriptures declare that when the devil lost the temptation with Jesus he departed "for a season." You must understand in your life that you can put the devil on the run, but it will only be for a season. He will return to challenge your faith. He will return to challenge the anointing that resides within you. Your job is to maintain such a close fellowship with God that you are prepared each time that the enemy launches an attack. And every time he shows up, demonstrate your spiritual growth and development by defeating him with the Word of God.

The more knowledge of the Word of God you have, the more battles you can successfully win against the enemy. This is why it is important to hear the Word, study the Word, meditate on the Word, and most importantly obey the Word. Many people are more dependent on other people than they are on their true source of power and victory which is the Word of God. I encourage the saints to learn how to walk in victory for themselves as opposed to always depending upon others.

There are times that the Word of God will serve as a shield and sanctuary in the time of trouble. All hell can break loose around us, but we won't be affected by our environment. The Hebrew boys with their strong faith are prime examples. The Bible tells how they were thrown into a fiery furnace. This was a real fire, because the men who threw them in perished in the fire. However, these Hebrew servants were protected by the presence of God. The king came and looked down in the furnace and was amazed that: 1) the men were still alive, and 2) that they were not in the fire alone.

That has been my testimony for years! I have gone through many fires (emotional, physical, financial, relationship, spiritual, and the list goes on…) but God has always been right there. I believe that He has been there first because He is God and He is everywhere. I believe that He has also been there because He made a promise never to leave me nor forsake me. But, thirdly I know He has been there because I am a praiser. Yes, praise is what I do. And God likes praise. He likes it so much that He makes His presence manifest when His people praise.

It is a good thing to be like the Hebrew boys. Several points should be considered: 1) they went into the fire willingly, 2) they remained in the fire triumphantly, and 3) they came out of the fire victoriously. These are traits that should be evident in our life.

How many of us go willingly into a fire? Not many. If anything, we are running, hiding, and praying not to go through anything. Our prayers get longer and our praise gets louder! "Lord, please help me!" and "Oh, Jesus!" Somehow, we hope that we can get God to change His mind regarding certain tests, storms, and trials. Scripture teaches us that it is not our emotions that move God. But, it is our faith that moves the hand and the heart of God. We must learn that going through makes us stronger. We should be made better and not bitter because of our trials.

If our steps are ordered by the Lord, we must learn that just as there are mountaintops, there are also valleys that must be trod. God has a way of directing our lives in paths that give Him glory and confound flesh. We must be people of faith and learn to trust that God knows what is best. If the Lord is truly ordering our steps, why would we "rebuke" the Lord? Sometimes, we must learn to accept our plight in life and know that God is yet able to bring forth the deliverance that we need. We must have faith as the Hebrew boys. We must walk with our chests pushed out and our heads held up high, with the testimony in our mouth, "Our God is able to deliver us! And, if He does not deliver us, it does not mean that He can't!"

The Bible says that the king looked down into the fiery furnace and saw the three Hebrew boys walking around. They were no longer bound, but they were free from their shackles. And then the king saw a fourth person in there that was said to be like the Son of God. Did not God promise you that He would always be there for you? He said, "Lo, I am with you even to the ends of the earth." We must walk in victory even in the midst of what we are going through, knowing that we are not walking alone. We must have a praise in our mouth in good times and bad times. Walking triumphantly in the fire means you must walk with your head up. You must ignore whatever is going on around you and trust the God who said, "He would never leave you nor forsake you." Walter Hawkins recorded a song many years ago that had great truth to it: "Don't Wait Till The Battle's Over – Shout Now!" That is so true because you do know in the end you are going to win. You must believe that you are already a winner.

And as you exit the fire, you definitely must have the physical characteristics of the Hebrew boys. What is so astonishing is that the Word of God declares that: not a hair of their head was singed and they did not even have the scent of smoke on their clothes. This speaks volumes into my heart and mind. First of all, I cannot allow what I go through to affect my future adversely. I do not want to look or smell like what I have gone through. I want to come forth as pure gold!

I shared during a New Year's Eve Service to the congregation the following thought: Whatever you have been through, if it was God that was with you and brought you out of it, you ought not to look like what you have been through. I think of women who have been through horrible abusive relationships. Some women have come out of these tragic ordeals bitter and bruised. But, there are some who trusted God, praised God, and obeyed God. These women have come out of the same ordeals as some of their other sisters, but they have been made better not bitter. I believe that it is God's will for any adversity that we suffer to bless us and not curse us. We should advance and not retreat. We should come out of whatever the situation is and be made better.

The Hebrew boys did not suffer damage because of their trial. They can serve as examples unto us. You must keep a positive attitude in your trial knowing that God is your keeper. One tactic that saints must adopt is to speak the best and believe the best. Even if you don't feel like a victor, never let it come out of your lips. That is exactly what the devil wants. Your words have power and are just like seed sown. If the devil can get you to begin talking negatively about your situation, he immediately begins to water the seed that you have sown. But, if "God's praise" is continually in your mouth, the devil has nothing to contaminate. He is defeated by your praise.

You can come out of your trials unscathed and uncontaminated by the devil and his devices. You can even be like Job and end up more blessed than before you ever went through the trial. It is all in your attitude. It is all in your praise. It is all in your worship. Invite the Lord into your trial with you and He will (as the old hymn said) *"comfort, strengthen and keep you. Jesus will carry you through."*

AN ATTITUDE ADJUSTMENT

Praise is an attitude adjustment. Praise ignores facts and aligns itself with truth, *"...Thy Word is truth."* **John 17:17** Praise does not lose itself in the midst of predicaments and problems. But, in the midst of whatever is going wrong, praise still declares that everything is alright. Not that it is going to be alright, but it's already alright.

I recall how I deal with my children when they have a minor injury. Some may feel as though it is heartless, cold, or callous; but I feel that it builds faith and strength. If they scrape their knee or bump something and come running and crying, they already know my response. "Stop crying!" Their response, in the midst of their tears is, "But it hurts!" And my reply simply is, "Are the tears healing it or making it any better?" They whimper out

> Praise dictates the posture of our body and our soul. We stand when others fall. We bounce back when others never recover. We smile when others frown. We think ourselves happy, when others resolve to be sad.

a sheepish, "no." Then I tell them to be quiet so that they can tell me what happened and give me an opportunity to treat it.

I feel that our praise is the discontinuance of whining and complaining. Our bellyaching about situations does not bring resolution to anything. When we allow negative emotions to get the best of us, the end results are usually physical complications (headaches, ulcers, high blood pressure, stress) and relationship maladies (mistreatment of innocent bystanders, loss of valuable time with loved ones). We can do much better without either. We must begin to change our attitude and believe that our answer and deliverance are in our praise.

Your attitude has to change. Your facial expression, your emotional tone, your disposition all have to demonstrate that all is well. This type of attitude requires a person's mind to be changed and to be conditioned by the Word of God. You cannot think like the world and expect to receive positive, godly results. Your mind has to be changed by the power of God. Thoughts are powerful. And thoughts precipitate actions.

"I beseech you therefore, brethren, by the mercies of God, that ye present your bodies, a living sacrifice, holy, acceptable unto God which is

your reasonable service. And be not conformed to this world: but be ye transformed by the renewing of your mind, that ye may prove what is that good, and acceptable, and perfect, will of God."
Romans 12:1

In this passage of scripture, Paul is directing the saints at Rome to make some inward and outward changes. And the most important thing about these changes is that it is God's will for the changes to be made. In light of our present discussion on praise, we must acknowledge that this scripture supports the principles that we have shared. We know that praise is an outward expression of an inward attitude.

First of all, Paul says to present our bodies. This means that we have to willingly give of ourselves. Real praise should not be forced from an individual. But real praise is where you make a decision that I will *"...shew forth the praises of Him who hath called me out of darkness into His marvelous light."* **I Peter 2:9**. No one has to encourage or prod you to do it. But, because you love the Lord with all your heart, soul, and mind, you have no problem clapping your hands and giving God the glory. When you realize who you used to be and how the Lord changed your life, you don't mind singing or shouting.

When you think about where you were headed (to hell), and how the Lord changed your eternal destination (heaven), you don't mind leaping, dancing or doing whatever it takes to give God praise.

Secondly, Paul says to present our bodies as a *"living sacrifice."* This is interesting. In the Old Testament, whenever sacrifices were brought to the altar, they were killed. This means that once they were placed on the altar, they remained there. However, if you take into consideration a *"living sacrifice,"* you might see a different picture. Imagine yourself lying on an altar and all of a sudden a fire is started beneath the altar. What would you do? Or imagine yourself lying on an altar, and all of a sudden someone approaches with a knife in order that your blood would be shed. What would you do? You already know the answer. You would attempt to get up! That is the major problem with a *"living sacrifice."* A living sacrifice has the ability or power to not remain on the altar. This is what makes our challenge greater. Paul is saying that we must make a conscious decision to get on the altar and stay there. This requires faith and steadfastness.

Paul continues by exhorting us to not be conformed to the world. This means that we have to be different. We cannot be like everyone else and still please God. We must be different from others in our praise, in our faith, in our lifestyle. It is so easy to murmur and complain because of the challenges of life. But, when one's mind is adjusted, you will find that it is just as easy to speak the best, believe the best, and accept only the best.

The Scriptures declare, *"As a man thinketh in his heart, so is he."* **Proverbs 23:7.** This simply gives foundation to the adage that your *attitude determines your altitude.* The mind is a powerful organ. When a person is focused, determined, and confident there is nothing impossible. Remember, the people at the tower of Babel: God confused their speech.

"And they said, Go to let us build us a city And a tower, whose top may reach unto heaven: and let us make us a name, lest we be scattered abroad upon the face of the whole earth. And the Lord came down to see the city and the tower, which the children of men builded. And the Lord said, Behold the people is one, and they have all one language; and this they begin to do: and now nothing will be restrained from them, which they have imagined to do. Go to, let Us go down, and there confound their language, that they may not understand one another's speech. So the Lord

scattered them abroad from thence upon the face of the earth: and they left off to build the city. Therefore is the name of it called Babel: because the Lord did there confound the language of all the earth: and from thence did the Lord scatter them abroad upon the face of all the earth." **Genesis 11:4-9.**

There is nothing impossible to a group of people when faith and unity come together and are made manifest. I think about awesome praise services where the Lord moves by His Spirit in such an awesome way that words are inadequate to explain. This happens when the atmosphere is set. I believe this is why prayer and praise are so key to a powerful worship experience. When people of like-minded hearts come together with one intent and purpose, the power of God is unleashed in such a way that needs are met and even heart desires are fulfilled.

The Scriptures even support this in **Matthew 18:20**, *"For where two or three are gathered together in My name, there am I in the midst of them."* The "in my name" portion of that verse does not simply mean that you showed up for church or you just happened to stop by bible study. But, when believers gather with a heart and mind focused on honoring the Lord, then things happen. A great example is when Pastor Benny Hinn holds a service, there is much praise and worship involved. And, when the atmosphere is set, the Lord shows up and He begins to "show out." Healing, deliverance, restoration and much more happen when prayer and praise have brought forth a powerful worship atmosphere.

Some people think that is all about Pastor Hinn, but it is not. He has learned that when he can get the people to adjust their attitude anything can happen. Praise must rid your mind of the present condition or state of affairs in your life. Then praise takes you to a place of intimacy with the Father called *worship*. When the worship atmosphere is set, God's Spirit is made welcome. And where the Spirit of the Lord is present, truly there is liberty.

IS THERE A RIGHT PLACE?

Where is the appropriate place to praise God? Is there a place where praising God would be considered improper or out of place? Is there a place that is off-limits or out of bounds for praise to be exhibited? Is there a place that we should not praise God?

To answer these questions, we must remind ourselves of the effects of praise. A songwriter once penned the words, *"When the praises of God are going up, then the blessings come down."* I expanded upon that thought to line up with the Scripture verse where *God inhabits the praises of Israel* **(Psalm 22:3). "When the praises go up, then the BLESSOR comes down".** That's right! Our praise ushers in the very presence of God.

> Wherever you want God to show up is the appropriate place to praise Him.

Not only does praise usher in God's presence. But, praise also serves as a witness and testimony to others of WHO God is and WHAT God has done! Praise also serves as an encouragement for us. When we remind ourselves of the magnificence and majesty of our Sovereign God, we are comforted and strengthened in the inner man.

So, as we reflect upon the appropriate place to praise God – I must submit that wherever you want God to show up is an appropriate place to praise Him. In the sanctuary of course, but also in the house – from the living room to the bedroom to the bathroom to the kitchen to the washroom. In the car, on the job, on the street, at the grocery store, at the mall – are all appropriate places to praise God. We need to invite God to show up in all of these places even more so than the grand efforts we make to get Him to show up in the sanctuary. It is not that we do not need Him in the sanctuary, but His presence is often more needed in those other places where our flesh has a tendency to attempt to control our spirit man.

Think about it! Where do you tend to lose your temper, say things that are not friendly, or do things that are unbecoming of a Christian? Of course not at church! Now I am not saying that you will never lose your temper at church. That is another chapter in another book. But, we must admit that when we are at church, we have a tendency for some strange reason or another, to regard and revere that place more than other places. Even though, we all admit that God is all places at all times, based on our actions we oftentimes act like we have amnesia.

Wherever I am is where I need God to show up. So, my life becomes a habit of praise. I learn to tell Him how much I love Him and thank Him while just driving down the street. Before I get out of my bed in the morning, I begin to reflect on His goodness and I wave my hands in worship. Or while walking down the hallway on my job, I just start humming a praise medley because I know that God is there with me. In the grocery store, I just say "Thank Ya!" at the checkout counter when I realize that my total is the exact amount I have in my pocket. "God is a good God. He is good all the time. And all the time, He is good!"

Praise is a testimony. Many people do not know God in the pardon of their sins. And many do not have a personal relationship with Jesus Christ as their Lord and Savior. So, when others see us unashamedly praising God in public places it is a great witness tool. Now, I believe things should be done decently and in order. I don't believe you have to start speaking in tongues and laying hands on folk and dancing down the aisles in the grocery store because grapes were on sale for 99 cents. But, I believe that you should be able to express your confidence and pride in your God wherever you may be. You should always be ready to boldly declare that it is God's mercy and grace that has brought us through. You should be a ready witness to always give God the glory, honor, and praise before those who would rather give credit to man.

When I go to a sports event, I do not have a problem telling God thank you. Because when my team wins, I believe God gave them the victory and I give Him glory for it. Now, I know some of you are reading and saying so what do you say when your team loses? I still give God praise. And I proclaim, God is such a good God, His Word has come to pass, He allows His sun to shine on the just as well as the unjust! I refuse to let an opportunity pass where I don't give God the glory.

Other people may call you strange or crazy. But, you will find it is those same people that when they get in trouble and need prayer or a Word from the Lord they will be calling on you. Because of your demonstration of faith in God your number is the one they will dial. It is your door on which they will be knocking. They will be looking for you because they know that you are connected to God. How did they know this? They knew it because you were not ashamed to praise God. They knew it because of all of the times you boasted on God and His power. They knew it because even when you had challenges and difficulties they saw a smile on your face as you gave God a "yet praise." They knew it because of your lifestyle of praise.

The old saints used to sing a praise song, *"The more I praise God, the better I feel,"* and that is the honest truth. The more that I praise Him, the more encouraged I am. Praise lifts my spirit. Praise adjusts my attitude. Praise changes my disposition. Praise does wonders for my emotions. It makes me laugh when I want to cry. Praise turns my mourning into dancing. Praise is medicinal. It can not only heal broken and wounded spirits, but it will even bring physical deliverance.

I have gone to church in pain and in the midst of the praises, the pain left. I can recall on a particular Friday night I was so tired but I felt impressed in my spirit that I needed to get to church. My back was hurting and my body was telling me I needed to lie down. But, I obeyed my spirit and pressed my way. When I arrived at the church the praise service was already underway. People were singing, rejoicing, and dancing. I had one of those Psalm 100 experiences. I began to tell God thank you as I walked through the door. And by the time I got to my seat, I had sat my Bible down and I was leaping up and down because I was so excited just to be amongst the saints in praise. Well, wouldn't you know, the back pain I experienced earlier of course had miraculously gone away. And after service, it did not return.

I have given God the sacrifice of praise and when I came out of worship, He had spoken to my heart regarding situations and circumstances in my life. He gave me the answer when He showed up for worship. That is one of the beautiful things about worship, when God speaks. God gave me some lyrics that really blessed me and whenever the choir sings the song, others are blessed immensely. The song is called "Tarry In His Presence." And that is exactly what God wants us to do. We must praise God until we get to worship. And when we arrive in worship we wait on God to simply be God.

The lyrics of the song say, *"Come and bow down before the King of Kings. Come and adore the Lord of Hosts. For His glory and His splendor are too wondrous to tell. Tarry in his presence. Tarry in His presence. Wait, now worship the Lord."* Those are powerful words as the people are encouraged to praise God and bask in His presence. When God's Spirit manifests in a place you cannot help but to worship Him. Worship is an intimate fellowship with God. The verse of the same song continues, *"There are times when the Lord wants to speak to you. There are times when He wants to commune only with you.*

Be still and know that God is God. Wait, now worship the Lord." That is awesome. Worship is private and personal. When you allow yourself to praise God and His Spirit manifests in your life, God makes deposits in our hearts. There are things that He wants to say that won't come through the prophet or the evangelist. There are some things that God wants to say and do, which only involve you and Him.

I have praised God at the house, on the job, in my car, and every place that I gave God praise He showed up. This pleases God. When we learn to praise God anywhere and everywhere we can experience new dimensions of God's glory that hitherto fore we had not experienced. That is what God wants to do. He does not want you to have a place in your life that He is not welcome. But, wherever you are, He wants to be invited.

WHEN IS THE RIGHT TIME?

David said in the Psalms, *"I will bless the Lord at all times, his praise shall continually be in my mouth."* **Psalm 34:1** There are two times that we should praise God: when we feel like it and when we don't! Our praise must not be based upon our feelings, but our praise should be based upon who God is, what God has done, what He is presently doing, and how we expect His omnipotence and omnipresence to bless us in the future. Because praise ushers in God's presence, it is relevant and important to always have *a praise* in our mouth. We need God to manifest in our life everyday, every hour, every minute, every second, and every moment. Yet, we must do what it takes to bring forth the manifestation.

> Even though, God will honor an emergency praise – His heart's desire is continual fellowship.

I am reminded where David commanded his soul (his emotional man) to *"Bless the Lord, Oh my soul and all that is within me."* **Psalm 103:1** How many times have you not "felt" like praising God? How many times have life's pressures weighed you so far down that you did not have the emotional stamina to do anything but cry, and be in pity. This is a great time to praise God!

There are times that you must put yourself in check. No matter what may be going on in the present and no matter how bleak or dismal the future looks, I dare you to reflect on what God has already done in your life. When you begin to reflect on what God has done, and how undeserving of His goodness you are, you would have no choice but to give Him praise. In the 103rd Psalm, David begins to reflect on the benefits that God afforded him. David, a man after God's own heart, is determined to bless God for who He is: the forgiver, the healer, the redeemer, the blessor, and the satisfier.

Just take a few moments and consider your life. When you were lost in sin, who was the one that loved you enough to forgive you even before you asked for forgiveness? **Romans 5:8** declares, *"But God commendeth his love toward us, in that, while we were yet sinners, Christ died for us."* That is awesome. If God did nothing else for us, the fact that we are saved through the shedding of His only begotten Son's blood on Calvary is reason enough to praise Him all day and all night for the duration of our days. Give it a try. Just think about the mess you were in. Think about how you were on your way to hell. Think about how you tried to change yourself, yet you failed in all of your own attempts. And then begin to praise God for bringing you out of darkness into His marvelous light. Begin to praise God for allowing His love to lift you from sinking sand. Give God praise for changing you and making you a new creature.

I can recall so much of my life – in the church, but there was no church in me. I do not have the testimony of some who had no knowledge or exposure to God or His church. Quite the contrary, I was almost born in church. As long as I can remember, church has been a regular part of my life. The blessing in this is how while I was living a sinful life, God had already decided to allow His Son to die for me. This is mind boggling. That God would love us to that extent even in His omniscience.

As I reflect upon my sordid past, I am encouraged even the more to praise God. I can recall even as a teenager how I would sing God's praises on Sunday morning and go out and smoke weed and get drunk on Sunday evening. It was nothing but a good, compassionate and forgiving God to keep me in the midst of a messed up life like that. Even throughout college, I had a zeal but not according to knowledge. I knew about God but I really did not know Him. My life was filled with smoking, drinking, illicit sex all the while I was still "in church." I am so grateful for that blessed Friday night in September when the Lord became real to me. I actually stopped running from God and began to run towards Him. And in His love for me, He received me.

God knows our risings and fallings. God knows even the intents of our hearts. God knows when we are being truthful with Him and He knows when we fabricate and tell lies. However, this knowledge does not stop God from loving us enough to provide salvation to us. His unconditional love forgives us of the past, the present, and even things to come. He is a forgiver.

David remembered that it was God who healed all of his diseases. In **Exodus 15:26**, God promises that if we hear His Word and obey His Word, *"... I will put none of theses diseases upon thee, which I have brought upon the Egyptians, for I am the Lord that healeth thee."* And today, because we are in covenant relationship with God, we can stand on God's Word found in **I Peter 2:24**, *"by His stripes ye were healed."* How many times have you been sick and had to depend upon God to bring forth your healing? I have nothing against medical doctors, because I believe that whatever knowledge they have came from God. Also, understand what they are. If you notice the sign on their door it reads, "practicing physician". That is exactly what they are: practicing! They do not have all knowledge. But there is one, Jesus Christ is the Great Physician, who knows all and can heal all.

We should praise God for being the healer. There are instances where doctors have walked in hospital rooms and given up. However, many of those same patients have turned their face to the wall (like Hezekiah) and received another lease on life from the Lord. If you don't know God as a healer, I challenge you to lie in your bed and sincerely call His name. If you praise Him, He will show up. The Florida Mass Choir recorded a song some years back entitled *"Come On, In My Room."* The scenario involved a woman who invited the Lord to come in and she testified that Jesus was her doctor and His prescription was what she needed for her healing. God is still working miracles today. He is still healing today. Praise God in advance for your healing.

Understand that praise and faith work together. So, find healing scriptures to support your confession. Begin to recite them and mutter them, but most of all believe them. Reciting God's Word is saying what God has already said.

You must remind yourself that God's Word is not like your word. You can say something of your own will and accord and it is mere conversation, just words. However, God's Word is immutable. It is more powerful than man's word. God even declared in **Isaiah 55:11**, *"So shall My word be that goeth forth out of My mouth: it shall not return unto Me void, but it shall accomplish that which I please, and it shall prosper in the thing whereto I sent it."* Isn't that wonderful? When God's Word goes forth it will not return back to Him until it has done what He says. That is why I encourage people to say what God has said. So, if God sends forth His Word to heal you, your healing has to manifest.

Also, you must understand the importance of muttering God's Word. Muttering is where you repeat His Word over and over as you focus on the intent and power of what you are saying. What this does is causes you to meditate, ponder, consider. This is important because it causes your spirit to be awakened to the power of God's promises. The more you say it and believe it, the more you think about it and line up with it, the more your faith is exercised to bring the manifestation. But, until it happens you should just praise God in advance for the manifestation of your healing that is nigh.

We should praise God for being our Redeemer. Understand, that when Adam and Eve sinned, the entire human race fell. We were *"born in sin and shapen in iniquity,"* according to **Psalm 51:5**. But thanks be to God, His love for us surpassed our sin. **Titus 2:4** tells us, *"Who gave Himself for us, that He might redeem us from all iniquity, and purify unto Himself a peculiar people, zealous of good works."*

I remember when I was a little boy, my mother used to save S&H Green Stamps. She would put them in little books. And when she had saved enough stamps, she took the stamps to the store and used the stamps to purchase what she wanted. An interesting point to be made is the fact that money could not be used to make the purchase – only the stamps. How similar is that scenario to our own lives. We were bound in sin and Jesus Christ came to redeem us. The only payment for our redemption was his precious blood. Nothing else could pay the price for our souls.

One of the most memorable passages of scripture paints the entire picture: *"For God so loved the world, that He gave His only begotten Son, that whosoever believeth in Him should not perish, but have everlasting life."* **John 3:16**. We should praise God for loving us enough to pay our ransom. We had a debt we could not pay. *"The wages* *of sin,"* according to **Romans 6:23,** *"is death, but the gift of God is eternal life through Jesus Christ our Lord."* We should glorify the Name of the Lord for blessing us with the gift of eternal life.

Margaret Pleasant Douroux wrote an anointed song some years ago, based upon **Psalm 124:1**, where she asks a simple yet profound question. *"If it had not been for the Lord on my side, where would I be?"* Now you can fill in the blanks concerning where. And every time you fill in a blank "a praise" should manifest in your body. You could have been dead. You could have been locked up in jail. You could be lying in a hospital bed with an incurable disease. You could have been in a mental institution and not even know your name. You could be standing on a street corner addicted to drugs. But, look at you! And to tell the honest truth, some of those "coulds" really ought to be "shoulds". But, God in His love for you, looked beyond your faults and failures and "bought you back." Yes, a marred vessel, but he purchased you anyway so he could make you over again. You were a dim light, but he purchased you so He could rekindle your fire. You were a dilapidated house, but He purchased you so He could make renovations and make His dwelling place in your body.

Praise God for the roof over your head. Praise God for the shoes on your feet. Praise God for the clothes on your back. Praise God for the paycheck you receive. For all of God's blessings – praise Him!

God is a blessor and a satisfier. **Psalm 37:4** encourages us to, *"Delight thyself also in the Lord, and He shall give thee the desires of thine heart."* This verse tells us the easiest way to get things from God. Some other translations of this verse tell us to: "Be happy with the Lord, and He will give you the desires of your heart." (God's Word). "Enjoy serving the Lord, and He will give you what you want." (New Century Version). "Keep company with God, get in on the best." (The Message). Now, just think about it, if I praise God, God is pleased and He rewards my praise. Not only will He supply my needs, but as I delight myself in Him, He will even bless me with my wants and desires. Who would not praise a God like this?

Praise is always relevant. All the time is the right time to give God praise. When we are under pressure our praise seems to gravitate towards two forms: either fervent or non-existent. Some people allow their circumstances to have so much weight, that they refuse to bless God in the midst of what they are going through. It does not matter what we face, God is just and God is good! We cannot allow the enemy to shut our mouths and place our praise on "lockdown" because of what we are facing. It is at this time that we must show the devil whose side we are on.

There are some who praise God fervently when they are faced with crisis situations. They realize that they have no power or control in their situation and begin to totally depend on the only hope and help they know. This type praise knows no boundaries or limitations.

Eventhough, God will honor an emergency praise – His heart's desire is continual fellowship. He wants a daily praise. The Gospel Music Workshop of America recorded a song a few years ago, "All day long, I've been with Jesus." This is the relationship God wants. All day long, our lips should utter praise. Just like He walked through the garden with Adam, now that we have been redeemed and been given full access to the throne room, He wants to commune with us on a daily basis. We should experience the lyrics of that Sunday School song, "And He walks with me, and He talks with me, and He tells me I am His own, and the joy we share…" That is the ideal praise – anytime, anywhere!

WORD BASED PRAISE!

How do you do it? How do you smile and praise God when your mind, body, even your circumstances and environment say you shouldn't? It is quite simple. It is a matter of choice. You must choose to be happy. You must choose to be alright. It does not matter what may exist in reality, you have to learn to look beyond what you see, what you feel and even what you know (or what you think you know). You must learn to look through the eyes of faith. You must learn to operate like **Romans 4:17: "...calleth those things which be not as though they were."**

> When you know what God's Word says and you confess what God's Word says, then you can see change erupting.

Praising God is a matter of faith. Faith in who He is, faith in what He can do. For what can you believe God? For what can you trust God? Well, praising God at what may seem to be an impossible time is really quite easy. You must know what God's Word says. You must believe what

God's Word says. You must say what God's Word says. When you know what God's Word says and you confess what God's Word says, then you can see change erupting. You must remember that: 1) you have the power of life and death in your tongue, 2) the words you speak are spirit and life, and 3) when you ask God and do not doubt, God will bring the answer that you need. These are promises that God has given through His Word.

Take a look at some scripture verses that address some common issues and concerns that we as Christians are faced with on a daily basis. If you can believe these verses, confess these verses, then you can receive the manifestation of these verses in your life.

Addictions –

"Know ye not that ye are the temple of God, and [that] the Spirit of God dwelleth in you? If any man defile the temple of God, him shall God destroy; for the temple of God is holy, which [temple] ye are."
1 Corinthians 3:16-17

Adversity –

"Many are the afflictions of the righteous: but the Lord delivereth him out of them all." **Psalm 34:19**

Sexual Sins –

"But fornication, and all uncleanness, or covetousness, let it not be once named among you, as becometh saints;" **Ephesians 5:3**

Tests and Trials –

"That the trial of your faith, being much more precious than of gold that perisheth, though it be tried with fire, might be found unto praise and honour and glory at the appearing of Jesus Christ:" **1 Peter 1:7**

Sickness –

"They shall take up serpents; and if they drink any deadly thing, it shall not hurt them; they shall lay hands on the sick, and they shall recover." **Mark 16:18**

Poverty –

"[When] the poor and needy seek water, and [there is] none, [and] their tongue faileth for thirst, I the Lord will hear them, I the God of Israel will not forsake them." **Isaiah 41:17**

Spiritual Warfare –

"For though we walk in the flesh, we do not war after the flesh: (For the weapons of our warfare [are] not carnal, but mighty through God to the pulling down of strong holds;) Casting down imaginations, and every high thing that exalteth itself against the knowledge of God, and bringing into captivity every thought to the obedience of Christ;" **2 Corinthians 10:3-5**

Bible Study

"Study to shew thyself approved unto God, a workman that needeth not to be ashamed, rightly dividing the word of truth. But shun profane [and] vain babblings: for they will increase unto more ungodliness." **2 Timothy 2:15-16**

The first step is knowing God's Word. David wrote, *"Thy Word have I hid in my heart, that I might not sin against Thee."* **Psalm 119:11** This is a very powerful statement. When we don't praise God – we are in sin. Oops! I did not mean to offend anyone, but let me explain. *"…Whatever is not of faith is sin,"* **(Romans 14:23)** according to the Word of God. And praise is simply faith being expressed. So when I refuse to praise God, basically I am refusing to manifest faith. And if I am not manifesting faith, then what am I manifesting?

We need to know what God's Word says about Who God is, What God can do, and Who we are in Him. When we know these things and stand on God's promises regarding these things, we can move the hand of God by our faith. For our faith is not based upon fleshly motives, but upon the truth of God's Word which is immutable. God's Word cannot lie and does not change.

Secondly, you must confess God's Word. Confessing God's Word demonstrates your belief in it and also sends the Word out into the earth realm and into the spiritual realm. Don't forget that God's Word cannot return void. If you want a surefire way of defeating the devil in your life – the Word of God is your key. Jesus did it and it worked for Him. He is our example setter. So, remember you have a foolproof method of defeating the devil on a daily basis.

In each of the areas mentioned on previous pages and in any other area where you may be facing challenges – the Word of God is your key to victory. Utilize the Word to praise your way to deliverance. The Word works! Self-help books may fail. Counseling may not work. Friends and family may even let you down. But, God's Word will always prevail.

Let us look at some sample Word-based confessions you can make that give praise to God and also bring victory to your life. Confession is powerful. Remember, your salvation even became manifest by *"the confession of your mouth."* **Romans 10:9**. When you confess God's Word you do three things: 1) You send God's Word into the earth realm which has to accomplish what God decides for it to accomplish because it cannot return void, 2) You bring life or death to a situation because you have that power (authority) in your tongue, and 3) You activate faith by agreeing with what God says and this pleases God and moves the hand of God.

Remember, your life purpose is to glorify God. When your life lines up with His Word, God gets the glory. The devil wants us to live raggedy lives. He wants to have us accept living beneath our spiritual privileges and rights. But, we have learned the more excellent way.

Try making these Word-based confessions on a daily basis…

Addictions – I thank God that my body belongs to God. I do not belong to myself. God purchased and redeemed me with His Son's precious blood. So, no longer do I have to allow Satan and his demons to control my mind or use my body. I am free from addictions because my body is God's temple. God lives in me. I move and breathe at His command. And I confess that my spirit, soul, and body are under the control of the Holy Spirit.

Adversity – I thank God for the sun that shines and for the raindrops that fall. I am encouraged and not discouraged when adversity comes. My faith is in Jehovah – who is my deliverer. There is no hardship or calamity that will come my way that God will not come forward and bring me out. As God delivered Job, He will deliver me. As He brought the Hebrew boys out, He will also bring me out without damage.

Sexual Sins – I thank God that because my body belongs to Him, I will keep it sexually pure. I am free from the spirit of fornication, adultery, lust, homosexuality, and all perverse and unholy acts that the enemy would present in my life. Because I am a born again, blood washed child of God, I am free from the control of images and even suggestions that the enemy may present. My mind and body are now in alliance with my spirit which is pure and holy.

Tests and Trials – I thank God for all things in the Name of the Lord Jesus. There is no trouble or trial that can come in my life that God has not already provided victory for me. God is my deliverer. God is my strong tower. God is my defense. God is my strength. I confess that I am not stressed out by challenges that come, but I am encouraged to know that God is simply allowing a testimony to be built from the tests that I go through.

Sickness – I thank God that He is my healer. There is no sickness, disease, or infirmity that can come upon me that He will not have mercy upon me and bring my total recovery. I plead the blood of Jesus' against all sickness. I stand on God's Word that by His stripes I am healed. And because I am a praiser, I turn my face to the wall as Hezekiah did and thank God in advance for turning my situation around.

Poverty – I thank God for delivering me from the spirit of poverty. I thank God that all my needs are met. I thank God because I am a consistent tither and a faithful giver, His Word will come to pass in my life. The devourer is rebuked, heaven's windows are open, blessings more than I have room to receive are coming, and good measure, pressed down, shaken together, and running over men do give into my bosom. I praise God that when it looks bleak, my financial breakthrough is on the way. I am confident to know that because I am the righteous, I will never be forsaken and my seed will never beg for bread.

Spiritual Warfare – I thank and praise God for victory in every battle. Every spiritual attack that is launched against me and my family is brought to naught. Greater is He that is in me than the devil in this world. My opposition is not in the flesh, but in the spirit. I am armed for battle. I have on the whole armor of the Lord. And the Word of God in my life causes strongholds to come down, imaginations and high things that exalt themselves against the knowledge of God are cast down, and every thought is brought into the obedience of Jesus Christ.

Bible Study – I thank and praise God for the importance of the Word of God in my life. I thank God that he keeps my body and mind alert to receive wisdom and knowledge. I thank God for a teachable spirit. I thank God that as I study His Word, I correctly understand, interpret, and communicate His Word. It is His Word that I have hidden in my heart that keeps me and strengthen me.

I challenge you to do it. I challenge you to confess the truths of the Word of God. And as you make these confessions, believe these confessions, and line your actions up with these confessions you will see the manifestation of God in your life as never before. You will see the miraculous. You will experience the supernatural. You will even feel the intangible. You will begin operating in a brand new spiritual dimension.

We have gone through a season in the church where many people have been made aware of God's covenant names. But, we must do more than zealously recite them and place them as high points in our songs, sermons and prayers. We must actually know and believe that God is who His Word says He is.

God is Jehovah Jireh. He is the God that provides. God is Jehovah Nissi. Yes, He goes out before us as a banner and He reigns in victory. God is Jehovah Shalom. Yes, He is the God of peace. And He brings peace that passeth all our understanding. God is Jehovah Roe. He is our Shepherd, as He was David's, and we should not want. God is Jehovah Tsidkinu. He is our righteousness and we stand complete in Him.

All of this is wonderful to say. It is great information to know. But, what good does it do you to say it and know it and miss the benefits of it? That is one of my greatest concerns in the church. We are always singing songs about *"I've Got the Victory!"* But, where is the manifestation? Don't get me wrong. I am not talking about "material possessions" as proof. But, I am talking about where your spirit and countenance actually change. I mean where your smile and happy face last longer than the praise service. It is easy to get excited and jump on the emotional bandwagon during a hyped praise service. But, what happens when you leave the church? What happens when you are home alone? What happens when there is no one to talk to? What happens when the mailman only brings bills and the checks are few and far between?

This is when your spirit must lay hold on your confession of victory and your countenance must change. There is no room for complaint. There is no time for depression. There is no place for doubt or fear. You must simply do what you do – and that is Praise!

Those actions that may seem uncomfortable or maybe even embarrassing or inappropriate, it is time to allow them to take center stage. Remember, God is your audience. He is waiting and watching for your display of praise. So, when my hand wants to go in my pocket, I raise it in the air. When my feet want to hold tight to the floor, I began to make them move in a rhythmic praise dance to my King. When my mouth wants to just be quiet, I open it and began to talk about the goodness, greatness and glory of the Father.

Knowledge is so very important to seeing God's Word manifest. **Hosea 4:6** says: *"My people are destroyed for lack of knowledge."* If we are to survive and prosper we must learn the Word, confess the Word, obey the Word, and then see the Word manifest in our lives. Our praise must be based on God's Word and not our fleshly attitudes and emotions.

WHEN I ROSE THIS MORNING

I woke up this morning, and as I began to ramble around the house, I began to reflect. I realized that God really had been good to me. He had been better to me than my family or friends. He had been better to me, than I had even been to myself. He was still being good to me. I mean, I began to reflect on who I was and all I had done. I even thought about the things that He had directed me to do, and I still had left undone.

> We are survivors not because of anything we have done, but because of God's purpose for our life.

Yet, in the midst of my humanity, God in His divinity had compassion on me. And I questioned myself and I asked, Why? Why would he bless me? Why would he keep me? Why would he extend His favor unto me? Why would he heal and deliver me? And then it came to me like a rushing mighty wind – for HIS Purpose.

I began to praise God for His purpose. The verse of Scripture, *"All things work together for good to those who love Him and are called according to HIS Purpose."* **Romans 8:28**. I realized that I was a survivor not because of anything I had done, but because of God's purpose for my life. That is so awesome.

What does it mean to be called? Well, without the aid or assistance of a dictionary, in laymen's terms it means to be summoned or requested to move from one position to another position closer to the one initiating the call. In the natural, when you were a child and outside playing if you heard a loud voice calling your name you knew that you had to move! If the voice was mama saying, "Johnny, come home," you knew that you had to stop your agenda and march to her beat. In the spirit realm, those of us who are born again were *"called out of darkness into His marvelous light."* **I Peter 2:9**. Isn't that wonderful? God in His love for us summoned us from the darkness of sin into the realm of holiness with Him. That means that we immediately made a decision to "cease and desist" our life of sin and move to the direction of His voice to obey His Will.

His call was a call of love. He called us out of sin because He loved us so much. That alone is reason enough to praise Him. Just the fact that we no longer have to die in our sins, but we have been given abundant life now and eternal life later, is more than enough reason to praise the Lord.

Each of us has a "call" on our life. Oftentimes, people get confused. Some feel that when they experience a spiritual awakening with God, that they have been called to the "preaching or pastoral" ministry. That is not always the case. Just because we are Christians we ought to be able to lead someone to Christ. Just because we are Christians we should be able to expound on the Sunday School lesson and bring understanding to a group of people. Just because we are Christians we should be able to pray and get results. Just because we are Christians we should be able to lay hands on the sick and see them recover. We should take authority over the demons and cast them out. Just because we are Christians we should be able to stand before a group of people and bring encouragement, hope, joy and faith. However, when some people develop these traits, they feel that God has "called" them into a special ministry.

I can recall when I accepted the call of God on my life. I had already been functioning as a spiritual leader. I was teaching Sunday School at church. As the director of a local community choir, I also initiated and led a home bible study. During these times (we call them the good old days!), we saw God move in miraculous ways. There were people who accepted Jesus as their personal Savior. Some people were filled with the Holy Ghost. There were healings that took place. And even a few deliverance sessions were held where people who had been tormented and afflicted by evil spirits were freed by the power of God.

God has called each of us into ministry. We do not have to wear a robe, preach behind a podium, or hang a cross around our neck to validate our "calling". But, what we must do is be faithful to our calling. The hymn writer wrote: *"To serve this present age, my calling to fulfill, Oh may it all my powers engage to do my Master's will."* That is what we must do. We must commit our spirit, soul and body to do the will of God. We must study His Word, be sensitive to His Spirit, and walk where He leads us. When we can accomplish this in our lives, then our love for Him is made manifest.

The Scriptures exhort us in **John 14:15**: ***"If ye love Me, keep My commandments."*** Does this mean when we disobey Him that we do not love Him? I would think not? How many of you have ever disobeyed your earthly parents? Did you love them any less? Of course not! But, as you grew and matured you realized that the true way to demonstrate your love and respect for your parents was to walk in obedience. The same is true with God. We must grow in Christ and become more mature. Our obedience is the proof or fruit of our mature love.

I can recall as an adult how my attitude towards obedience has evolved. There have been instances where my father has made requests of me that I really did not want to adhere to. But, because he is my father and I realize the blessing and benefit of 1) honoring your parents, 2) obeying your elders, and 3) showing submission in love, I complied without complaint.

Always admonish yourself from **I Samuel 15:22**, **"...*To obey is better than sacrifice.*"** I can recall growing up; my mom used this phrase so much. She would say, "Obedience is better than sacrifice." I used to hate to hear her say it. It seemed like every time I would do something wrong and suffer because of it, she would rattle off this phrase. I did not realize that she was quoting from the Bible until I was an adult! But, she would use that statement to encourage me to simply do what was asked of me and that negative consequences would be minimized. Makes sense now! Made no sense then! I just figured she wanted to just run and control my life. But, really what was happening was she was utilizing her wisdom and experience to try and give direction to my life so that I could become successful.

God operates pretty much the same way. He allows the Holy Spirit to speak into our lives. God wants us to be successful. The Holy Spirit's job is to lead us into all truth. However, many times because of the struggle between our spirit, soul and body – we don't always follow or obey. Paul gave an excellent example of the struggle in the Book of Romans.

> ***"For that which I do I allow not: for what I would, that do I not; but what I hate, that do I. If then I do that which I would not, I consent unto the law that it is good. Now then it is no more I that do it, but sin that dwelleth in me. For I know that in me (that is, in my flesh,) dwelleth no good thing: for to will is present with me; but how to perform that which is good I find not. For the good that I would I do not: but the evil which I would not, that I do."* Romans 7:15-19**

How many times have you felt like this? Even at times of physical, emotional or spiritual struggle we must learn to praise God. This is part of the devil's tactic to distract us from God's true purpose. When I can grasp the revelation of "all things working together for my good," then I can praise God no matter what is going on. It does not matter what's going on in me or around me. Because God has already worked it out! Hallelujah!

What does "All things working together for my good "really mean? It simply means that because God is supreme and in total control, He causes all events to work toward the fulfillment of His ultimate purpose. When it rains, He allows us to grow. When the sun shines, He allows us to be warmed and strengthened. When it snows, He allows us to rest and seek shelter that He provides.

A REAL PRAISE

What is a "real praise?" A real praise is a sacrificial, uninhibited, and determined effort on the part of a believer to get God's attention. This chapter is for people with problems. To all of the "perfect" people – this chapter may not be for you. This chapter is for those who have struggled, are still struggling,

> A real praise can only occur when we demand that our soul and body line up with the convictions of our spirit man.

and yet are determined to stay on the battlefield. This chapter is for those who have been broke, are still broke, don't see any increase coming, but are determined to stand on the Word of God believing that prosperity belongs to you. This chapter is for those who have been sick, have prayed and got sicker, but yet know that God is a healer and in His time your healing will be made manifest. This chapter is for those who have struggled on the inside, are still struggling and don't know when deliverance will ever come. Yet, something down on the inside of you encourages you that deliverance is on the way.

The devil is our adversary. His job is to oppose us on every hand. To everything that you feel God has said "yes" to, the enemy brings reasons of "no". The major problem is that our flesh oftentimes aligns itself with the enemy. The devil says you are physically ill and then symptoms begin to develop in the flesh. If we are not careful, we will find ourselves lining up with what the devils presents. No matter how sick you are or how sick you get, you must continue to declare that Jehovah Rapha is still the God that heals you.

Let us take into consideration our make-up. We are spirit beings, with souls (mind, will, intellect, desires, etc.), and our spirit and soul are housed in a body. When God created us He said, *"Let us make man in our image, after our likeness:..."* This is an awesome decision that God made. God, the Triune God, in His Oneness made us just like Him. God, the Father, represents our spirit. For God in His truest essence is a spirit. And we also are spirit beings. God, the Holy Ghost, represents our soul. This is the part of God that demonstrates emotions. In **Ephesians 4:30**, the Bible admonishes us, *"And grieve not the Holy Spirit of God, whereby ye are sealed unto the day of redemption."* And God, The Son, took on the form of man and lived on the earth for 33 years where he experienced the same challenges and physical limitations that we experience today.

As we understand our make-up, we also understand the struggle that we sometimes have with praise. The spirit man which has been born again is always ready, willing and more than able to praise and honor the King. However, it is the other two parts: the soul and the body where we experience the greatest challenges. These are also the parts of us that listen to the false evidence that the devil propagates. A real praise can only occur when we demand that our soul and body line up with the convictions of our spirit man.

A sacrificial praise is a praise that costs something. It costs an offering of your time, talent and treasure. Time is so precious. It is a gift from God. Even though, God is not limited to the framework of time, many of the things He does are seasonal and if we are to benefit we must honor the timeline which God establishes. Many have missed blessings and opportunities because of a blatant disregard for time.

I can personally attest to dishonoring God by not valuing time. There have been points in my personal life and ministry where I knew that God was opening doors and because of my own slothfulness, I missed the opportunity that God had set up for me. We must be sensitive to the move of God's Spirit and understand what season we are in.

Regarding praise, we must give God of our time. We must be willing to sacrifice time and P.U.S.H. (Praise Until Something Happens)! Some people want to sing a quick song or two and sit down. But, keep in mind the objective and purpose of praise. We praise God not only to give Him the glory that He is due, but also to welcome His presence and enter a worship experience with Him.

I call it flirting with God. It is like walking down the street and winking across the street at someone to get their attention. God is saying, come a little closer. God does not want us winking at Him. God wants a personal, intimate worship experience that can only be obtained through deliberate and consistent intentional praise. There are personal things that God wants to invest in your spirit that only come when worship happens.

A real praise must be generated from a pure heart and an honest soul. God is looking for integrity and character. You do not have to be perfect. But, you must grow up in God to learn to be "real" with God." Your praise must grow in intensity from mere fleshly manifestations of hand clapping and toe tapping to a more intense offering of soul searching and heart rendering of gratitude. You must allow your praise to be strong enough and deep enough to take you to the intimacy of worship. Yes, you must not be afraid to go beyond the veil. God has given you access to the throne room, so learn to take your liberty and enter in.

God expects our praise to be exhibited through the sacrifice of our talents. ***"And whatsoever ye do in word or deed, do all in the name of the Lord Jesus, giving thanks to God and the Father by Him,"*** according to **Colossians 3:17**. When we do normal everyday activities, we should make certain that God receives the glory. Thank Him on your job. Students should thank Him in the classroom. Lawyers should thank Him in the courtroom. Doctors should thank him in the operating room. Parents should thank Him in the home.

And when God has blessed you to excel at a particular thing, you should practice giving Him praise, honor and glory for your ability. A singer should always publicly give God the praise when doing a great job. A basketball player should publicly give God the credit for the high scoring game or the MVP award he received. We are in error when we act like whatever we have done; it was because of our own doing. It matters not how many lessons you have taken, or how many years you have spent practicing and refining your skill. We must always remember, it was God that gave the gift in the first place. Also, it was God that blessed you to learn and perfect your gift.

A real praise constitutes three stages: a real past, a real change, and a real new man. When a person can go through these stages they can offer an "anyhow" praise. This is a praise where the devil cannot trap you into being silent because of your past. The devil cannot put your praise on "lockdown" because you may still be a work in progress. There are seven keys (or steps or stages) to an anyhow praise.

When God has brought you out of darkness and delivered you, you have reason and a right to praise Him. You must always remember where you have been and what you did when you were there. One of the popular call/response choruses says, "You don't know like I know…" and the respondents reply "What He's done for me." And another popular praise chorus is "Jesus I'll never forget what You've done for me." These type songs help you to remember that you haven't always been saved. And even since you have been saved you have not always been perfect. But, you know that it was God and God alone who saved you. He raised you. He filled you. He blessed you.

Key one to an "anyhow" praise is acceptance. Yes, you must acknowledge that you are a mess and you need help. You have to learn how to not live in denial. You must be true to yourself and not live in delusion. That was one of the good things about David; he knew how to acknowledge his sin or condition. Stop blaming the devil for everything. Take responsibility and understand what the Book of James **(James 1:14)** says when it discusses how, *"Every man is tempted, when he is drawn away of his own lust, and enticed."*

And after accepting who and what you are, step two is confession. You have to open your mouth and tell your dirt! You may be embarrassed. You may feel uncomfortable. But, you cannot keep quiet about the skeletons in your closet. That is one of the enemy's tactics. If he can keep you from confessing it, then he can always hold it over your head. But, this is the way to true deliverance. Release it and let it go. This does not mean that you have to get up in the middle of church and make a big announcement about what you did Friday night (smile). But, you should have some trustworthy saints (prayer partners) in whom you can confide and depend upon to pray with you regarding your confession and your deliverance.

Repentance is the third step. After acknowledging and confessing who and what you are and what you have done you have to despise it. You have to "hate the sin that made the Spirit mourn." Repentance is a turning away. This must start in the heart. Other people may not see it initially, but that does not mean that it is not real. That is another tactic of the enemy. He wants to keep you around people who want to always remind you of who you used to be. He wants to flood your mind with the notion that you cannot change. Well, the devil is a lie! You can change. And you have changed when you accept the blood of Jesus that was shed on Calvary's cross to cover your life.

This takes you to step four which is thanksgiving. You may not look delivered and you may not feel free, but begin to thank God for your liberty. Yes, faith it till you make it. Keep speaking and believing that you are free. And, thank God for freeing and delivering you. Now, you are ready to take the focus off of you and start praising God.

You are not just praising God for delivering you, but you must learn to just praise Him because He is God. Step five is praising. Praise Him every moment and with every breath that you take. The more time you spend focusing on who God is, the less time you will have for the devil to cloud your mind with who and what you used to be. When you can continue in this type praise, you move into worship.

Worship is step six. This is an intimate fellowship with God. Worship is very personal. It no longer focuses on you, your problems, and your environment. It is all about Him. It is all about Who He is, His power, His splendor, His majesty, His Awesomeness. And when you are involved in true worship, it takes you to what I call the "caught up" zone. You are so caught up that you lose sight and mind of the finite things and issues of your daily life. Problems and situations lose their power and control over your emotions. Sickness has to even release its hold over pain and suffering in your mortal body.

Don't play games with me. You understand where I am going. When you and your spouse are spending that intimate precious time it is private and personal. And when things get really heated up, the phone may ring but either you don't hear it, or if you hear it you ignore it and refuse to answer it. Someone may knock at the door, but because you and your mate are "caught up" you decline to respond to the knock. This is the way worship is. Worship totally engulfs your spirit, soul and body to the extent that you lose consciousness of the finite world around you. You are caught up in God's presence and power.

When believers enter and experience this type of relationship with God on an ongoing basis, deliverance is inevitable. You cannot continue to spend time with God and still be who you used to be. Deliverance is step seven. The Word of God decrees that "whom the Son makes free, is free indeed." When God's Spirit is present, liberty comes. Those who dare to walk in their deliverance are those who are not ashamed to live a life of worship and praise.

WHEN I THINK OF THE GOODNESS

"When I think of the goodness of Jesus, and all that He's done for me!" is not just a saying – but it is a way of life. Some days, when nothing is wrong, my mind begins to reflect on the goodness of the Lord. It is at these times that I engage in a reflective praise. You talking about a wonderful feeling! Just to think of His goodness and bask in the knowledge of Him being good to you, brings unspeakable joy. It is not that you even deserved His goodness. It is just a joy to know that God has been and still is good to you, just because He is God.

> When our vision is made clear we see that we have never been alone.

How often have you reflected on God's blessings in your life? How often have you stopped to just think about the favor of the Lord in your life? How many times have you realized that it was only His grace and mercy that brought you this far along the way?

No matter what happens in our life, the goodness of the Lord always shines through. He is a turnaround God. He takes dismal and dark situations and brings joy and sunlight. **Romans 8:28** encourages us by reminding us that *"all things work together for good to those who love God and are called according to His purpose"*. So, when bad things happen to good people, it is God who works things out to bring good out of bad situations. He is always working on behalf of those who are in covenant relationship with Him.

That is what covenant is all about. Two parties come together and bring to the table things that are beneficial to the other party. The awesome thing about our covenant relationship with God is that we are the "needy" partner. It is not like God needs us. But, it is us who need Him. For it is by Him that all things exist. Also, it is in Him that we live and even have our being.

And since we are the ones who really need Him, God allows situations that ensure our neediness. The Psalmist said that the steps of a good man are ordered by the Lord. Sometimes, He orders our steps through the valley of the shadow of death. But, because of our covenant relationship we fear no evil because He is with us. God in His love for us grants us conditional favor and blessings.

This helps to enhance our fellowship and relationship with Him. God gives us a reason to be in covenant with Him. Think about all of the **"If"** scriptures in the Bible.

> **Exodus 15:26** - *And said, If thou wilt diligently hearken to the voice of the LORD thy God, and wilt do that which is right in his sight, and wilt give ear to his commandments, and keep all his statutes, I will put none of these diseases upon thee, which I have brought upon the Egyptians: for I am the LORD that healeth thee.*

> **Deuteronomy 28:1-2** - *And it shall come to pass, if thou shalt hearken diligently unto the voice of the LORD thy God, to observe and to do all his commandments which I command thee this day, that the LORD thy God will set thee on high above all nations of the earth: And all these blessings shall come on thee, and overtake thee, if thou shalt hearken unto the voice of the LORD thy God.*

Luke 17: 6 - *And the Lord said, If ye had faith as a grain of mustard seed, ye might say unto this sycamine tree, Be thou plucked up by the root, and be thou planted in the sea; and it should obey you.*

Romans 10:9 - *That if thou shalt confess with thy mouth the Lord Jesus, and shalt believe in thine heart that God hath raised him from the dead, thou shalt be saved.*

Those are some awesome promises. God will honor His Word. Healing, blessings, answered prayer, and salvation are just a few of the many promises available to believers. But these examples are conditional blessings based upon our actions.

Hindsight is 20/20. You can always see clearly after the clouds are gone and the sun begins to shine. After the moon fades away giving place for the sun to dawn in your life, your vision is clear. When we are in the midst of situations sometimes we feel alone or forsaken. But, when our vision is made clear we see that we have never been alone.

Memory is a blessing and a gift from God. It is one thing that the enemy can not steal, kill or destroy. In the passing of a loved one, you can always remember the good times. In the move from one location to another, you can always remember the joys of the old house or neighborhood. And in the days of trouble and trials, you can remember the goodness of the Lord. He has brought you through dangers, toils, and snares before and He will do it again.

And as you look back, you don't have to wonder – you know how you made it over. It was God showing up and showing out in those critical times. When you felt alone, He showed up to comfort you. Yes, He rocked you in the cradle of His arms. When you faced an obstacle that seemed impossible, it was God that showed up as a miracle worker. When all hope seemed to be gone, He allowed the sun to shine a ray of hope on your situation. When you thought the bottom had fallen out, and you were sinking deeper in despair, He came through as your knight in shining armor.

If you made an attempt to count your blessings, you could not count them all. God has been better than good. He has even been better to you, than you have been to yourself. As you think about all of this, it is difficult not to praise Him. Your eyes may well up with tears as you consider His goodness. Your lips may begin to stammer and speak in a language you never learned, as you reflect on His mercy. Your hands may begin to make wave motions in the air, as you think about His favor that He has shown unto you. If you had ten thousand tongues, it would not be enough to praise Him!

POWER IN PRAISE

Many people do not understand that there is power in praise. Praise does not simply come forth as a loud noise and reverberate throughout the room. But, praise exits the earthly atmosphere and ascends into the heavenly realm. Praise gets God's attention. And when God's attention is secured, He manifests in the place where praise is being offered. **Psalm 22:3** declares that *"God inhabits the praises of Israel."*

> Praise is distracting, destructive and detrimental to the enemy.

Today, we as "spiritual Israel" must come to the understanding that God wants us to experience His visitation. When God shows up, the devil is shut down. God is omnipresent. That means He is all places at all times. However, what blesses me about God is how He can be in a place before we arrive, show up with us when we get there, and when we begin to praise Him, He enters in yet still! That is awesome. Have you ever been in a service where you know that the Lord was there because you could feel His presence when you walked through the door? But, as the service progressed it was as if He came in all over again!

I am reminded of a funny little skit that we used to do when I was a little boy at the AME church. We used to perform a play called "The Little Old Country Church". Well, one of the members named Sis. Mary had not been to church since her husband died. So, one day some of the church members went out to Sis. Mary's house to try and encourage her to come to church. She was quite reluctant. Her concern was who would care for her chickens while she was at church. So, the church members told her that if she would come to church, the Lord would watch after her chickens. Whew! They finally got Sis. Mary to attend church. But, lo and behold the service was highly anointed and the Spirit of God was moving through the room. One of the other ladies jumped up and shouted, "The Lord is here! The Lord is here!" What did she have to go and do that for? Sis. Mary immediately rose from her seat and exclaimed, "Well, if the Lord is here, who at home with my chickens?" Well, you guessed right, Sis. Mary ran right out the door and back home to see about her chickens. She did not realize that the God we serve can watch over chickens and be at church all at the same time!

Our praise has power. Praise is distracting, destructive and detrimental to the enemy. The devil does not want us to realize that our praise has power. This is why he attempts to deceive us and cause us to get off course in our pursuit of purpose and destiny. He knows the power of praise. That is why he attempts to keep us from utilizing praise as a weapon against him. He knows that if he can keep us from praising God, he won't be defeated.

There was an instance in **II Chronicles 20:20** where we see an excellent example of the power of praise. The people of God faced opposition from several enemies. But, King Jehoshaphat instructed the people to have faith and be obedient. As they went forth into battle, the only weapon they had to utilize was "praise".

In verse **21** of **II Chronicles 20**, the Bible says that *"he appointed singers"*. How strange that is! When you are facing a formidable foe, your basic instinct is to get your best advantage over your adversary. Remember when you were growing up, you would always take your big brother and all of your cousins to make sure you didn't lose the fight. In this Biblical instance, you would have thought that he would take the strongest men, the most experienced warriors and send them forth first. But, that is not what happened. He sent the praisers first!

This type of response is distractive to the enemy. When you are under attack, the devil expects you to retaliate in a fleshly manner. He does not expect you to respond with praise. So, when you begin to bless God and praise Him the devil is confused. The next time you feel like you are under attack from the enemy, start praising God. When you feel like cursing, start praising. When you feel like hitting someone, start praising. When you feel like getting even with someone, start praising.

The enemy expects you to operate in the flesh by taking flesh weapons to war. However, we must always be mindful that this is a spiritual battle and flesh weapons will not work. **Ephesians 6:12** reminds us, *"For we wrestle not against flesh and blood, but against principalities, against powers, against the rulers of the darkness of this world, against spiritual wickedness in high places. Wherefore take unto you the whole armor of God, that ye may be able to withstand in the evil day, and having done all, to stand."*

The enemy is distracted when praise comes forth instead of bitterness, anger, hurt, resentment, confusion, doubt, etc. The devil's intent is to defeat you. He knows that he really has no power or authority. He also knows that God has given you authority, dominion and power. So, his plan is to deceive you into relinquishing your rights. If he can make you feel like you have no power, then you will act like you have no power. And the end result to this is defeat for you and victory for him.

Just think about it. Take for instance, that your car is broken. If you are trying to get to work and you don't want to be late, what do you do? Your natural, carnal mind tells you to call someone for a ride, or catch a bus or cab. But, what if someone blessed you with a brand new car and it is parked in your garage. You were not aware of it, because when they tried to tell you, you were not paying attention. They even left the keys in the flowerpot on the front porch. But, you had to find a ride in the storm and rain just to get to work. Upon your return home, you checked your voicemail, and heard the other party asking how is your new car doing? You called them back to ask them what in the world were they talking about. Tell me how you felt when they explain that they already told you that they were blessing you with a car. But, evidently you were not listening.

The above passage may sound funny and seem a bit outlandish. But, we do God the same way all of the time. God is always speaking to us, equipping us, preparing us, and investing in us. Oftentimes, we do not even realize that what we need to walk in victory on a daily basis, God has already placed within us. But through our failure to hear the Word, read and study the Word, understand the Word, and obey the Word, we often find ourselves struggling through life.

The next time you get angry or upset, put yourself in check. Make a plan to distract the enemy. Instead of reacting or responding with your flesh, allow your spirit man to be in charge. I mean just start praising God right then and right there. Don't curse them out. But begin to bless God. Don't allow angry or mean-spirited words to flow from your lips. But begin to bless God. Don't allow your facial expressions to react in a negative way. But, begin to bless God. Don't even permit bad thoughts to linger in your mind. But, begin to bless God.

Praise is the exact opposite of what the devil expects when he does his best to hinder you and the will of God. You bring confusion to the enemy's camp when you start praising God. When the headache comes, wave your hands and tell God thank you. When trouble is on the job or in the home, open your mouth and tell God how much you love Him. When tragedy strikes or some unforeseen negative event occurs, just clap your hands and express gratitude unto God.

You will be surprised at how the offensive attack lessens when you begin to praise God. The devil is so distracted by your praise that he has to withdraw and regroup. An excellent example of defeating the devil is given by Jesus in **Matthew 4: 1-11.**

"Then was Jesus led up of the Spirit into the wilderness to be tempted of the devil. And when he had fasted forty days and forty nights, he was afterward an hungred. And when the tempter came to him, he said, If thou be the Son of God, command that these stones be made bread. But he answered and said, It is written, Man shall not live by bread alone, but by every word that proceedeth out of the mouth of God. Then the devil taketh him up into the holy city, and setteth him on a pinnacle of the temple, And saith unto him, If thou be the Son of God, cast thyself down: for it is written, He shall give his angels charge concerning thee: and in their hands they shall bear thee up, lest at any time thou dash thy foot against a stone. Jesus said unto him, It is written again, Thou shalt not tempt the Lord thy God.

Again, the devil taketh him up into an exceeding high mountain, and sheweth him all the kingdoms of the world, and the glory of them; And saith unto him, All these things will I give thee, if thou wilt fall down and worship me. Then saith Jesus unto him, Get thee hence, Satan: for it is written, Thou shalt worship the Lord thy God, and him only shalt thou serve. Then the devil leaveth him, and, behold, angels came and ministered unto him."

After Jesus had fasted for forty days and nights the Bible says he was tempted of the devil. Every attack that the devil launched, Jesus simply responded with the Word of God. Did you not know that quoting Scripture can be classified as praise? Remember, praise is bragging or boasting about who God is. When we proclaim Scripture that talks about who God is, it can be considered a form of praise. And because it is praise, it can distract the devil.

Praise is also destructive to the enemy and his plans. Praise weakens the enemy and his plans. Praise weakens the enemy's control. Remember, faith moves mountains but doubt brings forth and establishes mountains. Praise is faith in action. Praise ignores the natural and believes the supernatural. We must remember that our spiritual power is always greater than natural power.

When we effectively utilize praise in this warfare, the devil suffers defeat because he cannot accomplish his goal. I am reminded of one Sunday where I had an excruciating headache. I almost stayed home from church. But, the voice of the Lord spoke to me and told me that I needed to get to church for my healing. At this time, I was attended a small Pentecostal church and so you can imagine the noise level of the service.

As I made it to church, I sat midways towards the back. The singers were singing, the musicians were playing, the people were praising, and my head was banging. The devil began to talk to me and tell me that I should have just stayed home. It was as if He had perched on my shoulder and started whispering in my ear. "You know your head is hurting." "You know all this noise ain't good for your headache." "You know you tired anyway." "God, knows your heart, you could have stayed home and God would understand." Have you ever heard any of these sorry lines that the devil offers?

And at that very moment, I went on the offensive against the enemy. I realized that my deliverance was in the praise. I immediately jumped out of my seat and began clapping my hands and shaking my head. Now common sense would say to be very still if my head was hurting, but faith said "shake it away". And, I obeyed faith. And moments after I began to praise God, my headache left and I soon forgot that I had even had a headache. I know that God is a healer and a deliverer and my faith working through praise had moved His hand in my favor.

THERE IS A PLACE

There is a place in God that every Christian should long and desire to exist. There is a place that the Psalmist refers to as *"under the shadow of (The Almighty) His wings".* **(Psalm 91:1) Psalm 17:8.** It is a place of refuge and a place of protection. It is a safety zone. It is a place where troubles and trials have no power over the emotions. It is a place where all hell can be breaking loose around you, yet you are consumed with peace. It is a place where difficult and dismal days are present, yet your heart and mind are comforted and not alarmed.

> Praise is the transport mechanism to take you to that place in God where you experience the assurance of being kept and hidden by God.

"I have called upon thee, for thou wilt hear me, O God, incline thine ear unto me, and hear my speech, Show Thy marvelous loving kindness, O thou that savest by the right hand them which put their trust in thee from those that rise up against them. Keep me as the apple of

the eye, hide me under the shadow of thy wings, from the wicked that oppress me, from my deadly enemies, who compass me about." **Psalm 17: 6-9.**

The entrance to this special place is through the gates of praise. As praise ushers in the very presence of the Spirit of the Lord, the manifestation of His glory brings deliverance. Yes, the power of fear, depression, anxiety, worry, sadness, dismay have no authority or control when the Spirit of the Lord is present. There is nothing the enemy can do when God hides you.

God desires to hide us, protect us, cover us, keep us, and bless us. He hears our pleas and rescues us from our adversary when we call on him in faith! He reveals himself as Jehovah Shammah – "The Lord is there". That means no matter where you are or what condition you find yourself, if you call Him: He will show up and manifest Himself. He is Jehovah (God that saves). And whatever you need Him to be when He shows up, He will manifest Himself – your healing comes, your deliverance comes, your breakthrough comes, your prosperity comes, your favor comes. So, not only do you receive protection from the enemy when God hides you, but also you receive the blessing that you stand in need of when God manifests Himself in your situation.

If praise can lift burdens, then praise is what I need to do! If praise can relieve stress, then praise is what I need to do! If praise can instill hope, then praise is what I need to do! If praise can bring encouragement, then praise is what I need to do! If praise can take me from my problems and take me to the problem solver, then praise is what I need to do!

Remember, praise is not the end result. Praise is only the vehicle or transport mechanism to take you to that place in God where you experience the assurance of being kept and hidden by God. That place is worship. Worship is the indescribable experience of intimate communion (or fellowship) with God. This cannot be done in the flesh, but the spirit man must experience this.

"For they that are after the flesh do mind the things of the flesh; but they that are after the Spirit the things of the Spirit. For to be carnally minded is death; but to be spiritually minded is life and peace. Because the carnal mind is enmity against God; for it is not subject to the law of God, neither indeed can be. So then they that are in the flesh cannot please God. But ye are not in the flesh, but in the Spirit, if so be that the Spirit of God dwell in you. Now if

any man have not the Spirit of Christ, he is none of His." **Romans 8:5-9**

Everything that has breath can praise the Lord, however, we must move to a different level or dimension to experience worship. The scripture above shared with us how the flesh is carnal and is at war against the truth of God. However, when we allow our spirit man to come to the forefront, then we experience the sweet communion of oneness with God. We can have a worship experience that takes us away from the constraints of this temporal world and translates us into a spiritual plane where God makes spiritual deposits that the carnal mind could never understand.

Even in the Book of John, Jesus tells us, **"*God is a Spirit, and they that worship Him must worship Him in spirit and in truth."* John 4:24.** This verse gives us spiritual guidelines for true worship. Worship comes from the spirit man and not from the soulish or carnal man. Also, worship must be based upon the truth of God's Word. The spirit of man is the place where God's spirit resides. And when worship takes place it is man's spirit that is united in fellowship with God's Spirit. It is in this instance where we receive from God's Spirit spiritual deposits of wisdom, knowledge, revelation, miracles, blessings, and much more.

When we worship God, God's spirit does not give us foreign information but He clarifies what God has already said in Scripture. So, Christians should always understand that when they sense, feel or hear a message it must line up with God's written Word. *"God is not a man, that He should lie; neither the son of man, that He should repent; hath He said, and shall He not do it? Or hath He spoken, and shall He not make it good?"* **Numbers 23:19.** There are many young Christians who get confused when they hear different messages and all claim they are speaking what the Lord hath said. This is why we must *"Study the word"* as dictated in **II Timothy 2:15**, so we can *"rightly divide the Word of truth"*. God wants us to have a one-on-one personal relationship with Him. This requires that we study His Word so we can know His truths as he makes revelation in our life.

The spirit or heart of man is a special place. It is a place where things that don't make sense in the natural make perfect sense in the heart, especially a heart of faith. A true believer can experience things that completely confound the carnal mind. Some people don't have these experiences because they are always attempting to think things out or figure God out. That is impossible! God is God and we are not!

The blessed thing about a deep spiritual relationship with God is that He communicates with us during intimate fellowship which is worship. A key verse found in **I Corinthians 2:9-10** states, ***"Eye hath not seen, nor ear heard, neither have entered into the heart of man, the things which God hath prepared for them that love Him. But God hath revealed them unto us by His Spirit: for the Spirit searcheth all things, yea, the deep things of God."*** Worship provides us the awesome opportunity to experience God in such a way that the human mind cannot conceive or even perceive.

That is the place I want to live. I want to live in that special place where I have daily communion (fellowship) with God. When I worship God in the Spirit, I am better able to deal with things in the natural. God's Spirit directs me and teaches me God's will, purpose and plan. His Spirit shows me how to be victorious over the enemy and his tactics.

OUT OF YOUR COMFORT ZONE

Have you ever been in a place where you knew that should praise God, yet your comfort zone would not allow you? Have you ever been ashamed to praise God because of the people around you? How many times have you wanted to just wave your hand or say amen, but you got scared and just held your peace. When we allow the enemy to silence us "even in a strange land", we invite the enemy's presence and ignore God's desire to manifest His presence and power.

It is so easy to be in the midst of a bunch of loud, radical, rambunctious saints and praise God. I mean we are creatures of assimilation anyway. How easy it is to lift your hands when everybody else's hands are lifted? Everybody around you is making noise and jumping, isn't it so easy to just jump right in and join the bandwagon. But, how easy is it to be a "Shouting John". I am reminded of the man in Pastor Shirley Caeser's song who would get happy at church and

> Praise that ignores your surroundings, environment, or atmosphere pleases God.

the church leaders came out to his farm to reprimand him. John did not care where he was or who was watching. His reply to their admonition about him making "all that fuss" in their quiet church, was "Hold my mule, and I'll shout right here!"

That is the type praise that gets God's attention. Praise that ignores your surroundings, environment, or atmosphere pleases God. Especially praise that ignores other people will take you to that place of worship. This is the time that you should be focused on getting God's presence to be made manifest and others' presence to be made unaware.

I can recall the early days of salvation. There were times that I could feel myself doing things that I had never done before. But fear would grip my heart every time I would attempt to move a muscle. You must remember, I was raised in a Methodist church. And, it was a reserved Methodist church. We knew who would shout, what time they would shout and what they would say and do when they did it! So, for me to hardly consider doing more than clapping my hand, patting my feet and nodding my head was incomprehensible.

I used to think (along with countless others) that something had to hit me in order for me to praise God. If I just did it on my own, I was being fake or hypocritical. What I failed to realize was that I was really being fake by sitting there thinking about praising God and refusing to do it. Praise is an action that we must initiate. And if it causes us to be a bit uncomfortable, so be it.

Consider this: How comfortable was Jesus when He was being beaten, mocked, spit upon, and scorned? How comfortable was He when he carried the cross that they were about to hang Him on up the hill to Calvary. How comfortable was Jesus when they nailed His hands and feet to that cross? How comfortable was He when they placed a crown of thorns upon His head and pierced Him in the side with a spear? How comfortable was He when He died for your sins and mine?

When I consider how uncomfortable He had been made just for me, it changed my perception about being comfortable in my praise. I grew to the point of ignoring people's perceptions, thoughts and comments. I also learned to ignore my own personal feelings about whether I was being or appearing silly or fake. I learned to just be thankful and express it. I learned to just be grateful and express it. I learned that it was okay to cry and nothing be wrong. I learned that it was okay to wave my hands and not want anything. I learned it was okay to holler "Amen" or

"Thank You Jesus" and people turn around and stare. I learned that it was okay to be the last person still standing after the song was over after everyone else had already sat down.

When God blesses you, you should praise him right then and there. When you think of His goodness, you should praise Him right then and there. When you remember that He alone is God, you should just praise Him for who He is at that very moment.

If you are in Walmart, and you find the item that you need at even less than a discount than you had prayed, praise Him! There is nothing wrong with lifting your hand and telling God "Thank You," right there in the middle of Walmart. If you are driving down the street there is nothing wrong with opening your mouth and telling God how much you love Him. You don't want anything. Nothing is wrong. You just started thinking about how good He is to you and how much you really do love Him.

Praise is not reserved for church alone. Yes, we should praise Him in the sanctuary. We should stand, lift our hands, lift our voices, dance, clap, and engage in every other action that glorifies God. But, when I am at home, I cannot put my praise on hold. When I am at work, God is still being good to me, and I have to learn how to give the

Lord praise even at the office.

Some people have a problem with praising God in public places. But, I am reminded in the Scriptures **(Mark 8:38)** where Jesus said, *"Whosoever therefore shall be ashamed of Me and of My words in this adulterous and sinful generation; of him also shall the Son of man be ashamed, when He cometh in the glory of His Father with the holy angels."* Just for clarification purposes, answer these questions...

What would you do if you were at a football game and your son ran 70 yards for a touchdown?

How would you respond if you were shopping at the mall and when you went to the check out, the salesperson told you that because you were the $1,000^{th}$ customer, you just won a $500. shopping spree.

How would you act if you went to the doctor for a follow-up and they told you the positive diagnosis that had been reported to you earlier was in error, and you are going to be alright and not be sick?

Even watching television, I have seen people uncontrollably loud and jubilant over somebody else winning a large sum of money. Question: How much of that money are they going to give you? Then why is it that you can be so excited about somebody you don't know and probably will never meet?

What would you do if you were driving down the street and your car miraculous stops without skidding or hydroplaning when the person in front of you is in a multi-car pileup, but you are spared the inconvenience and tragedy?

Or on a simple note, how would your respond if you were at the grocery store and the person in front of you allowed you to go before them because you were running late?

These are all instances where everybody knows you would respond with excitement, joy, exuberation, -- you got the point! Nobody would have to tell you to stand up and scream at the football game. Nobody could even try and sit you down, because you would yell and scream regardless. "That's my baby! That's my baby! He got a touchdown! That's my baby!" Because that is your son and you are proud of him and you are happy, it is right for you to express yourself. I do not have a problem with any of those emotions being displayed for your child. You should celebrate your child. You should be excited about your child's accomplishments, whether they are on the athletic field or in the academic arena.

And even in the simple instance of the person in the grocery store allowing you to go before them, you would respond, "Thank you." You would do it because it is the appropriate action to take. How much more should you tell God thank you even for what we call the "little things" in life.

I can recall going to the city league basketball games on Saturday mornings and watching my son. Of course when he shoots the ball and makes two points, I am excited. But, because he is my son, I get excited just seeing him on the court. He has my full attention and support when he is just running from one end of the court to the other. I am not glued to my seat. I am not quiet. I am not reserved.

What confuses me is the different response that Jesus receives versus all of this flesh. Who woke you up this morning? Who had your back during that trouble you were involved? Who healed your body when you were sick?

Now take into consideration, if we can show this much excitement about carnal things, how much more should we show the same (if not more) excitement about spiritual things. **Romans 6:19** says, *"I speak after the manner of men because of the infirmity of your flesh: for as ye have yielded your members servants to uncleanness and to iniquity unto iniquity; even so now yield your* *members servants to righteousness unto holiness."* If we can be happy towards the things of men, surely we should be able to transfer that same happiness to the things of God. Even in our praise: Don't stop dancing, just change dance partners!

There are people who will tell you that is doesn't take all that. Well, I beg to differ. If I can be excited about a man batting a ball over a fence that has no benefit to me, I surely can be excited about a man hanging on a tree and dying for me. We must learn to disregard our feelings of discomfort and focus on His goodness and mercy.

When you get out of your comfort zone you are in a place to get the *"exceeding and abundantly more than you could ask or think of"* because of the release of your faith (praise). When you are brave and bold enough to praise God and ignore your flesh, God is big and bad enough to bless your spirit and your flesh! Getting out of your comfort zone requires submission. Yes, you must completely surrender your mind and your body to God's will. That means you have to allow your spirit to be like King David in Psalm 103 and command your body and soul to "Bless the Lord, O my soul, and forget not all His benefits."

PRAISE IN SPITE OF YOURSELF

How many times have you fallen from grace, stepped out of the will of God, walked in sin and iniquity? For true believers, these times are generally followed by guilt, shame, repentance, hurt, frustration, etc.

> You have to start talking to yourself in the midst of your mess!

These vulnerable times are targeted by the enemy to discourage believers from praising God. The devil literally speaks to the mind, and causes people to think they hear themselves saying, "Now how you gonna praise God after what you did?" "You know you ain't right, so you might as well sit down and stop being a hypocrite." "No, don't lift your hands because you know they aren't holy."

There is a way out of that type of trap that the devil sets. For, the only real power that the devil has is what we allow him to steal or trick us out of. The way out is to confess and repent. Those actions kept David in good standing with God. David was loved so much by God. He even declared that David was a "man after my own heart."

David knew how to get things right with God. A wonderful passage of scripture is found in the first seventeen verses of **Psalm 51**:

> *Have mercy upon me, O God, according to thy loving kindness: according unto the multitude of thy tender mercies blot out my transgressions. Wash me throughly from mine iniquity, and cleanse me from my sin. For I acknowledge my transgressions: and my sin is ever before me. Against thee, thee only, have I sinned, and done this evil in thy sight: that thou mightest be justified when thou speakest, and be clear when thou judgest. Behold, I was shapen in iniquity; and in sin did my mother conceive me. Behold, thou desirest truth in the inward parts: and in the hidden part thou shalt make me to know wisdom. Purge me with hyssop, and I shall be clean: wash me, and I shall be whiter than snow. Make me to hear joy and gladness; that the bones which thou hast broken may rejoice. Hide thy face from my sins, and blot out all mine iniquities. Create*

in me a clean heart, O God; and renew a right spirit within me. Cast me not away from thy presence; and take not thy holy spirit from me. Restore unto me the joy of thy salvation; and uphold me with thy free spirit. Then will I teach transgressors thy ways; and sinners shall be converted unto thee. Deliver me from bloodguiltiness, O God, thou God of my salvation: and my tongue shall sing aloud of thy righteousness. O Lord, open thou my lips; and my mouth shall shew forth thy praise. For thou desirest not sacrifice; else would I give it: thou delightest not in burnt offering. The sacrifices of God are a broken spirit: a broken and a contrite heart, O God, thou wilt not despise."

Is sin wrong? Of course it is! All day and even at night! Sin is not God's will for our lives. Does God forgive sin? Yes He does. A great deal quicker than man! God hates sin, but He loves the sinner. God wants man to acknowledge his error and then to repent and walk upright.

Sometimes that process is easier said than done. Confession and repentance are acts of faith that take courage and strength to operate in. There are instances where the battle in your flesh is so strong and you feel as though you are losing that you consider giving up. Giving up is not an option. You can't give up! You have to start talking to yourself in the midst of your mess! And in these instances you will see how much power praise really has.

When you find it difficult to confess or repent – begin to praise God. Ignore those people who call you a hypocrite or a phony. Those are more tactics by the enemy to stop your praise and hinder your true deliverance. Don't even pay attention to your own mind. Do what the Bible says, if you have breath "Praise Ye The Lord!"

Start thinking on His goodness, and His mercy, and His longsuffering, and His tender mercies, and His kindness, and His favor that He has given. After thinking then begin thanking. Thank Him for how He kept you and never left you. Thank Him for allowing you to be a survivor and not a casualty. Thank Him for all the things that many often take for granted (waking up each morning, seeing the sunshine, having good health, going to work, etc.) And then thank Him in advance for what you are expecting.

You will find that praise ushers in deliverance. After praising God, your mind and heart will begin to intertwine and you will have a cognizance of your humanity and His divinity. This revelation will humble you and bring forth the confession and repentance that you desire in your heart to do.

As a believer, you must realize that the Word of God expressly states that "everything that hath breath should praise the Lord." That means: every liar that has breath! Every addict that has breath. Every drunkard that hath breath. Every cheater that has breath. Every whoremonger that hath breath. Every person who has stumbled. Every person who has made a mistake. Every person that does not fit the "accepted religious idea" of being worthy to praise God. Everything and every body. Praising God is simply acknowledging that God is good to all. Yes, God blesses the just and the unjust.

Some people have a problem with this theology. But, what you must understand – it is "their" problem. If God said "everything that hath breath" should praise Him, then who is man to argue with God's Word? Everything with breath can give God praise. Many times when those who may be out of God's will begin to praise God – their heart is convicted and deliverance comes.

Praise is a powerful agent. Regardless of who you are or what you are you must rise from the ashes of your despair and realize that you are a survivor. You are here because of God's goodness and mercy unto you. Even if you don't have it all together, don't allow your present state to hinder you from praising the One who is keeping and sustaining you.

Realize that praise is not about you, but it is about the King. Praise has nothing to do with the religious people at the church who may attempt to sit in judgment. Praise is not based on your situation or circumstance. Learn to forget about yourself and concentrate on Him and then give Him praise.

PRAISE: THE NATURAL THING TO DO!

Praise ought not to be considered to be a chore. Even though, sometimes we give what we call a "sacrificial praise." We really should reevaluate our terminology. A sacrificial praise is not praising God when you are tired or just don't feel like it. A sacrificial praise is where you give completely of yourself to Him. A sacrificial praise must cost you something.

> When we express praise during critical moments, God intervenes.

A common praise song recites, "We bring the sacrifice of praise into the house of the Lord...." What makes this praise sacrificial? Praise should be viewed as an offering or a gift. Praise should reflect our true emotions and feelings. And the more I love God, the more intense my praise should be. When I come to praise God, my cry is "All of me for all of Him."

When I offer myself completely to God, what I am saying is that I am willing to be a living sacrifice. My personal agenda is set aside to subscribe to the King's agenda. My own ideas are dismissed to adhere to the King's ideas. My own plans are postponed to expedite the plans of the King.

A willingness and heartfelt desire to praise God should be the norm for a believer's life. Every time you inhale you should remind yourself that it is God's mercy that even allows that breath. A sense of gratitude should manifest in your life by some sort of praise.

Do you remember the instance of David dancing with such little inhibition that he danced out of his clothes? When you consider the awesomeness, the greatness, and the goodness of God, your praise may reach the same intensity. I am not saying that you should dance out of your clothes. But, I am saying that your praise ought to be so intense and so intimate that no one or no thing around you really matters. Nothing should invade your praise.

When we reach this intensity in praise, our praise puts the "ignore" shield" up. Yes, everything and everybody around you lose their influence over and power of your attention. You are not distracted by past due bills, loss of employment, pain in your back, trouble in your home. Your praise is so focused that you literally ignore your circumstances and even your environment.

What do you do when you attend a church service? Do you immediately begin to thank and praise God or do you wait for a service or worship leader to prompt you? **Psalm 100:4** says, *"Enter into his gates with thanksgiving, and into his courts with praise: be thankful unto him, and bless his name."* I have taught the saints at our local assembly that when you walk through the door you should be telling the Lord thank you! Thank Him for keeping you while traveling. Thank Him for another opportunity to worship Him amongst the saints. Thank Him in advance for the Word that is about to be preached. Thank Him for what His Holy Spirit is about to do.

You don't need anyone to prod or provoke you into doing what should come naturally. Yesterday, He was good to you, so thank Him. Today, He will do even greater things for you, so praise Him! You have no need to fear tomorrow because He holds it in His hands, so you ought to bless Him. Even as you consider the power in His Name, you have no choice but to honor Him! **Acts 4:12** declares, *"Neither is there salvation in any other: for there is none other name under heaven given among men, whereby we* *must be saved."* And **John 14: 13-14** states, *"And whatsoever ye shall ask in my name, that will I do, that the Father may be glorified in the Son. If ye shall ask anything in my name, I will do it."* As you consider that your salvation, healing, deliverance, prosperity, blessings, favor, answered prayer, and everything else you need or even desire is made manifest through the Name of Jesus, you can not help but be excited about blessing His name.

I have experienced services where if I did not know better, I would have thought I was in an aerobics class or at the gym going through physical training. The praise leader is up front commanding and demanding the people to follow their instructions. "Stand up!" "Wave your hands!" Clap your hands!" "Leap for joy!" "Run!" "Jump" "Stomp!" "Scream!" It is so strange that people have to be prodded to do something that should just naturally occur.

Every time you "think" you should automatically and without delay "thank!" Think about His goodness, and thank Him for His mercy. Think about your past and thank Him for your deliverance. Think about your losses and failures and thank Him for His comfort. Think about your infirmities and diseases and thank Him for His healing. Think about your questions and thank Him for being the answer. Think about your unrest and confusion and thank

Him for His peace.

The Word of God says that praise is comely for the upright. This simply means that praise is normal, natural, and expected. We must grow to the point that praise is simply what we do! When we think of His goodness, our response should be praise. When we see His power made manifest, our response should be praise. When someone around us begins to praise God, our response should be to simply, without thought or planning, begin to praise God as well.

How many of us have to be told to breathe? How many of us are continually reminded to eat? How many of us have to have someone beside us reminding us of how to walk, talk, laugh, or cry? No, these are things that just come natural. We do them all on our own. Of course some of them are learned behaviors (walk, talk, etc.) but after we learn them we do not require continual coaching in order to do them. Praise should be the same. Yes, we should receive direction on how to praise God. God's Word is clear on the subject, and gives numerous examples of how, when, why, etc. regarding praise. But, we must also learn to take what we have been taught and operate in it.

We must grow to the point where biblical praise has been learned and practiced so much that it is simply what we do. We do not need any external stimulation. We do not need the cheerleader to pump us up. We just praise God because that is what we do. There should be no alternatives. There should be no options. There should be no other choices. We just do it because it is our natural response.

HOW TO DO IT!

There have been debates, lectures, sermons, seminars, even songs about "how" to praise God. Many well intentioned people have offended others in their zeal to follow their prescribed pattern. But, there is no "one set way" to praise God. Just understand that it is a verb, so that makes it an action word (smile). *You just gotta do something!*

Some feel that swinging from the chandeliers, running and making loud utterances are appropriate ways to praise God. There is nothing wrong with these actions, but praise is not limited to these extreme gestures. Saying that you love the Lord, waving your hand, even nodding your head and patting your feet are all appropriate ways to praise God. It just takes an external action/manifestation to qualify for praise. I can boast to my friends about who God is and that qualifies as praise. I can utter scripture verses about the goodness and mercy of God and that qualifies as praise. I

> Praise is an expression of the emotions, yet it is also a manifestation of the heart.

can sit in my seat and sway from side to side and that qualifies as praise.

Praise is an expression of the emotions, yet it is also a manifestation of the heart. Praise is not simply based on "how" I feel. If praise was only about feelings, God would not receive what was due unto Him. The heart must dictate praise. A prime example is **Psalm 103** where David commands his soul to bless the Lord. David had to talk to himself on various occasions. And in this instance, he had to take charge over his emotions and feelings. In other words, you must learn to ignore what else is going on and praise God "anyway!" Yes, you may be under attack, but yet praise God. Your back may be against the wall, but yet praise God. You may be challenged physically, financially, emotionally, or even spiritually – but yet praise God.

The Book of Psalms gives many different examples of appropriate ways to praise God. We should seek to employ as many of these ways as possible in our life. There are times we should clap our hands. There are times we should shout for joy. There are times we should make a joyful noise. There are times we should find stringed instruments and organs. (And learn to play skillfully). There are times we need to find some cymbals and high-sounding cymbals. There are times we should testify of

God's goodness, mercy and power. There are times we should leap for joy and then praise Him in a dance. There are times we should sing and pray. But at all times, we should "do" something that glorifies the Lord.

I have conducted seminars entitled *"Praise Into Worship"* to give singers, musicians, pastors, and congregations a better understanding of principles, practices, and procedures of biblical praise. The time spent in these sessions has proven beneficial. Not only do participants leave with a better understanding of the Word of God, but a renewed and determined mindset to praise God in a way that brings His manifestation and His glory.

The term "praise and worship" seemed a bit archaic and awkward to me. After studying the Word of God, I discovered that praise really was a transport mechanism that took us to worship. Thus, I coined the phrase *"Praise Into Worship."* Even during our Sunday Morning Worship services, the former praise service has been replaced by the more suitable title of *"Praise Into Worship,"* because praise into worship is what we actually do.

The praise leader has the awesome task of exhorting and leading the people of God into a corporate worship experience. Now, down through the years I have seen some strange and hurtful practices. I have heard praise leaders scold and fuss at the congregation. Much damage has been done to churches and people with such phrases as "You act like God ain't done nothing for you." and "You need to be ashamed of yourselves for sitting down on God like that!" If I am not mistaken, the Lord declared "With loving kindness have I drawn you." Praise leaders must be careful not to badger or berate the people. But the people should be lovingly invited to make the journey from praise to worship.

Not only should care be taken with words that are spoken, but also with the songs that are selected to be sung. I won't go into naming particular songs, but there are some songs that may be popular on the radio and may make the songwriter or artist a great deal of royalties but they do not necessarily glorify God or lend themselves suitable for a worship service. Just because a song has a nice beat does not make it suitable for worship service. Even lyrics that are cute and catchy, yet have no scriptural foundation should be avoided.

Songs should be selected first and foremost based upon scriptural integrity. If the song does not line up with the Word of God, it has no business being sung in the church of God. I don't care how smooth the rhythm or melody is or how "tight" the lyrics are. Praise songs, worship songs, spiritual songs must be based upon the unadulterated Word of God.

Songs should be used that minister to the emotional and personal needs of the congregation. Praise or worship leaders should be careful to understand the makeup of the congregation and select songs that will fit the particular groups of people that are represented. Hymns, choruses, spiritual songs, contemporary, traditional, all should be utilized in making the ministry all encompassing.

Following the leadership of the local assembly and the leading of the Holy Spirit are critical to things being done "decent and in order." Some churches have praise services that last about 10 to 15 minutes whereas other churches spend well over an hour in praise. Those leading the music must understand the guidelines and expectations of church leadership. I have heard some people say, "I just let the Lord lead me." I sometimes question that leading if God has set a spiritual leader in place whose directives differ from the "leading" that the musical leader is receiving. The correct protocol is to understand the vision and direction that the local pastor is leading the service and to allow the praise portion of the service to comply.

PRAISE AND FAITH

Praise and faith are intertwined. If possible, I would even personify them as identical twins. Or even more appropriately – Siamese twins. They are joined together and impossible to exist without each other. Praise must have faith present to be effective. And faith must include praise to be genuine. Praise and faith must co-exist.

> When we began to express God's power and God's awesomeness, then we can see how our faith moves God.

Praise in reality is an attitude adjustment. Praise smiles when there seems to be every reason present not to smile. True praise proclaims the goodness and greatness of God irregardless of present conditions. For example, Job, when he made the statement: *"Though he slay me, yet will I trust him..."* **(Job 13:15)**, he stood firm on his faith in God even though he was faced with adversity. So in other words, in order for praise to be effective it must incorporate the foundational essence of faith. And that is simply, believing and allowing your actions to support your belief.

What is faith? Faith is simply agreeing with God. If God said it, that settles it. Simple, huh? Now, we all know that Hebrews says that faith is the substance of things hoped for and the evidence of things unseen. So, in other words faith is substance and evidence. Faith takes what may not be detected by the five senses (taste, touch, smell, hearing, or sight) and brings manifestation by the sixth sense (feeling, understanding, will, desire, belief).

We all use faith everyday. Even in the natural, faith is an action that we all exhibit – saints and sinners alike. Take for example, a gambler – they operate in a kind of faith. Why do they gamble? They gamble because they believe they are going to win! After losing over and over, why would they continue gambling even at the expense of borrowing money from others to support their habit? They continue because they believe that the win they need to recoup everything is about to happen. Now this is not good faith, but it is a good example of faith in action. And it is this kind of tenacity that yields results. You would be surprised at the number of people who would experience healing, deliverance, prosperity, peace, etc. if they simply operated in uninhibited faith. Faith that has no boundaries or barriers will bring certain victory.

That is one thing that is so discouraging with some church folk. Their faith is not strong. They lose heart too quickly. **Galatians 6:9** declares, *"And let us not be weary in well doing, for in due season we shall reap, if we faint not."* We can not give up so easily. We must be strong and endure the tests and trials that are presented. One thing many fail to remember is that whatever you are going through can only last for a season. If it is dark, know that the sun will shine again. If it is winter in your life, know that spring and summer are on the way.

We must adapt the mentality of the farmer. The farmer sows his seed because he expects a harvest. Then he waters and cares for the seed by cultivating and monitoring the growth of the plant. When we sow the Word of God in a situation, our praise waters that seed sown. Our praise eliminates weeds. Our praise prevents drought. Our praise strengthens the plant. Our praise brings forth the fruit.

I did not grow up in a church that taught tithing. I was accustomed to paying dues and giving an offering. However, as I grew in God I began to learn the truth of God's Word. Tithing was a struggle for me at first. When I first started to tithe and realized that I was about to write a check for more than a hundred dollars, I started doing a double-take.

This was a challenge for me since I was accustomed to putting a dollar in church. Maybe on a special occasion, I would put five dollars in the tray. But, I had to grow in the knowledge of the power of obeying God's Word regarding tithing.

I can recall that tithing was the first spiritual conversation that my father and I had. My father is a giver. He will bless people and help people whenever he sees a need. However, we grew and learned that tithing to God and giving to others were to distinct and separate things. There are separate benefits for tithing and giving to the poor.

You cannot pay tithes two times and then wonder why you don't see immediate increase. Remember, we are living in a war zone. The enemy is going to do everything he can to discourage your faith. So, when you decide to release your faith in financial matters and start paying tithes – don't be surprised when challenges arise. Yes, you may get a pink slip on your job. Your lights may get disconnected. Your car may be repossessed. But, instead of allowing these distractions to discourage you – you must begin to cause your praise to encourage you. So when these challenges come, keep doing what you are doing until victory comes. Yes, keep paying your tithes and increase your seed offering. God is not sleep nor is He unfaithful. He sees and He knows. He will deliver.

When you are doing the faith walk, make sure your attitude is in check. **I Titus 6:6** declares, *"Godliness with contentment is great gain."* We must learn to be happy and that only happens when we decide it to be so. In order to be content, you must learn to live in "Contentment Land." It does not mean that you simply take what the devil is doing without saying or doing something. But, you must remind yourself of a strategy that will hinder the enemy's attack – "think yourself happy." **Proverbs 23:7** states, *"As he thinketh in his heart, so is he."* You must think that you are a winner.

Consider the woman with the issue of blood. She was down to her last chance. She had exhausted all of her resources. But, she began to talk to herself. She believed in her heart and confessed with her mouth that she could be healed by touching the hem of Jesus' garment. Her faith was under girded by praise. Now as you look at this woman's situation, you would probably say, "But, I don't see her praising God!"

We must come to term with the fact that praise is not just loud "Hallelujah's" and "Thank You Jesus's" But, praise is also confidence in God. When we began to really express God's power and God's awesomeness, then we can see how our faith moves God. She believed that her healing was in Jesus. She acknowledged that he was her healer. When we sing old hymns, like "How Great Thou Art," that is an expression of praise. And when we express praise during critical moments, God intervenes. Remember, praise gets God's attention and faith moves God's hands.

ABOUT THE AUTHOR

O'Neal Porter serves as the senior pastor at the Fellowship Church in Eight Mile, Alabama. He has earned degrees from The University of Alabama (Bachelor of Arts in Communications) and the Alabama State University (Masters of Education in Educational Administration). He is an active member of the Port City United Voices (Mobile, Alabama Chapter of the Gospel Music Workshop of America). He is also the founder and director of the gospel singing group: FAITH – Friends Are In the House. He and his wife, Sabrina, are the proud parents of: Kymberly Dawnique, Brooke O'Neal, Morgan Char'les and Charles Van James. He is an anointed teacher, psalmist, composer, choral director, gospel music workshop clinician and speaker. One of the special areas that God has gifted him is to lead *"Praise Into Worship"* seminars where he teaches praise teams, choirs and entire congregations biblical foundations and practical applications of entering into the presence of God. For contact information, address letters to: O'Neal Porter, P.O. Box 13125, Eight Mile, AL 36633. or e-mail him at soneal1019@yahoo.com or email the publisher at ohkneelpublishing@yahoo.com or call 251-219-4327.

CPSIA information can be obtained
at www.ICGtesting.com
Printed in the USA
LVHW060236100723
751979LV00004B/118